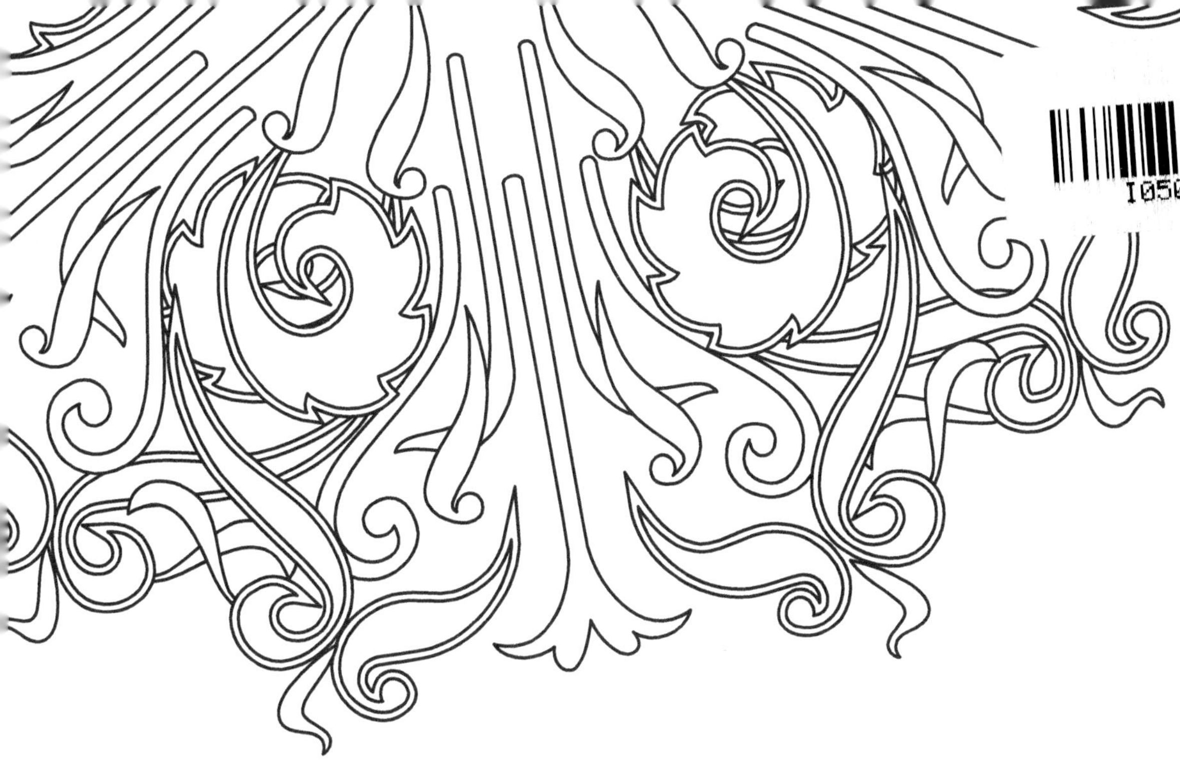

Floral and Gothic mandalas

Stress-relief coloring patterns for adults

Abbie Faith

ISBN: 1542723299
ISBN-13: 978-1542723299

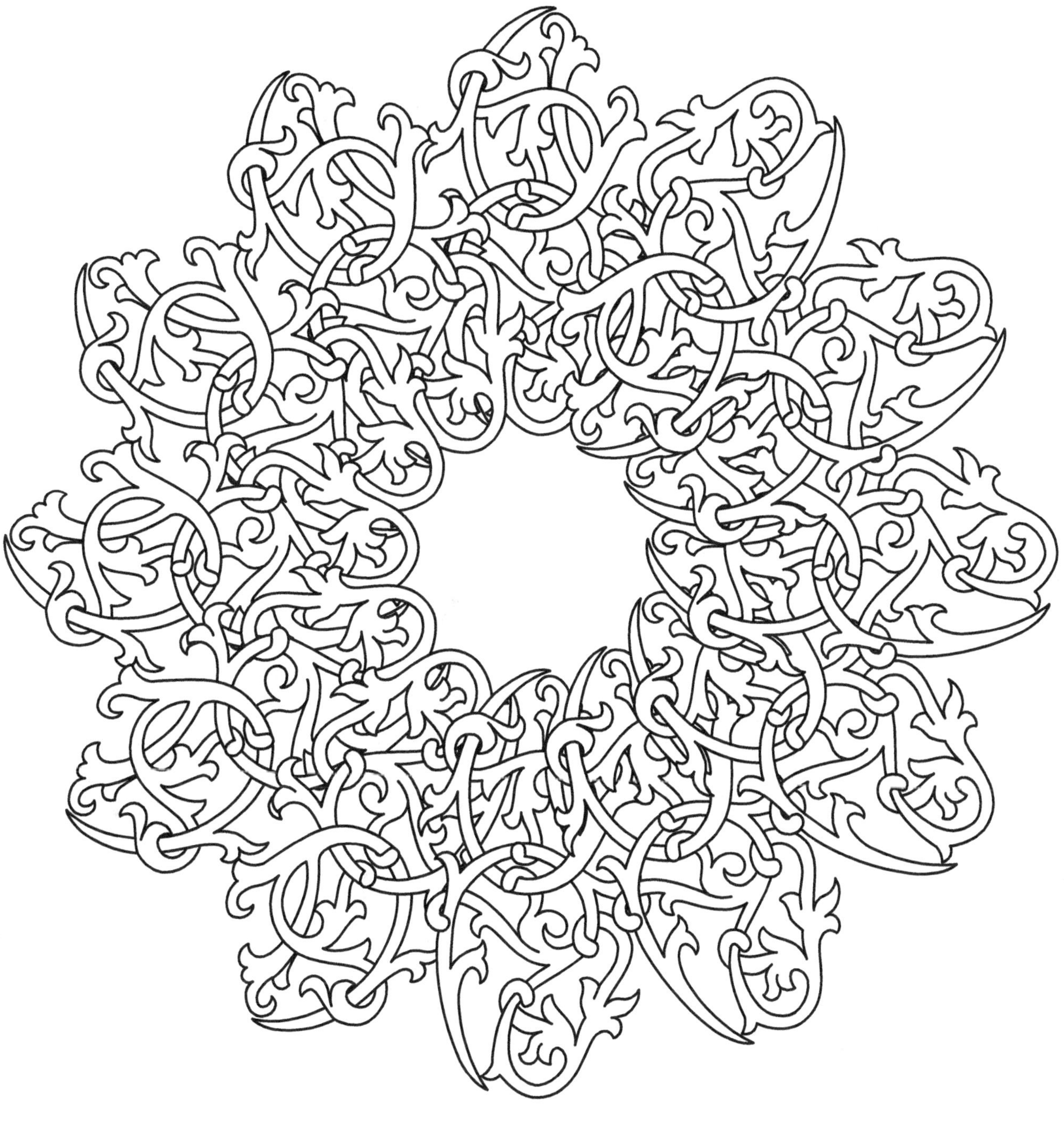

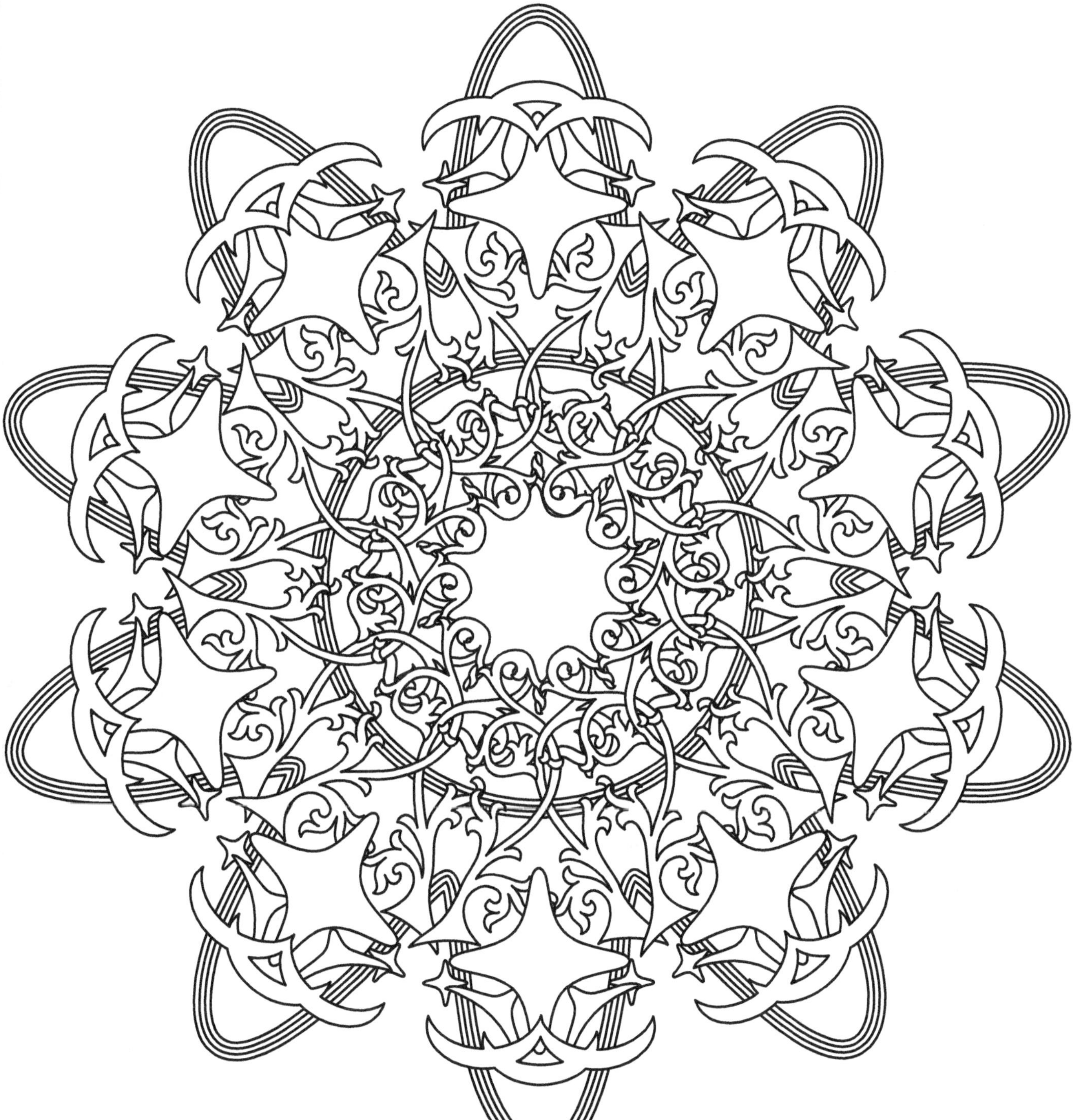

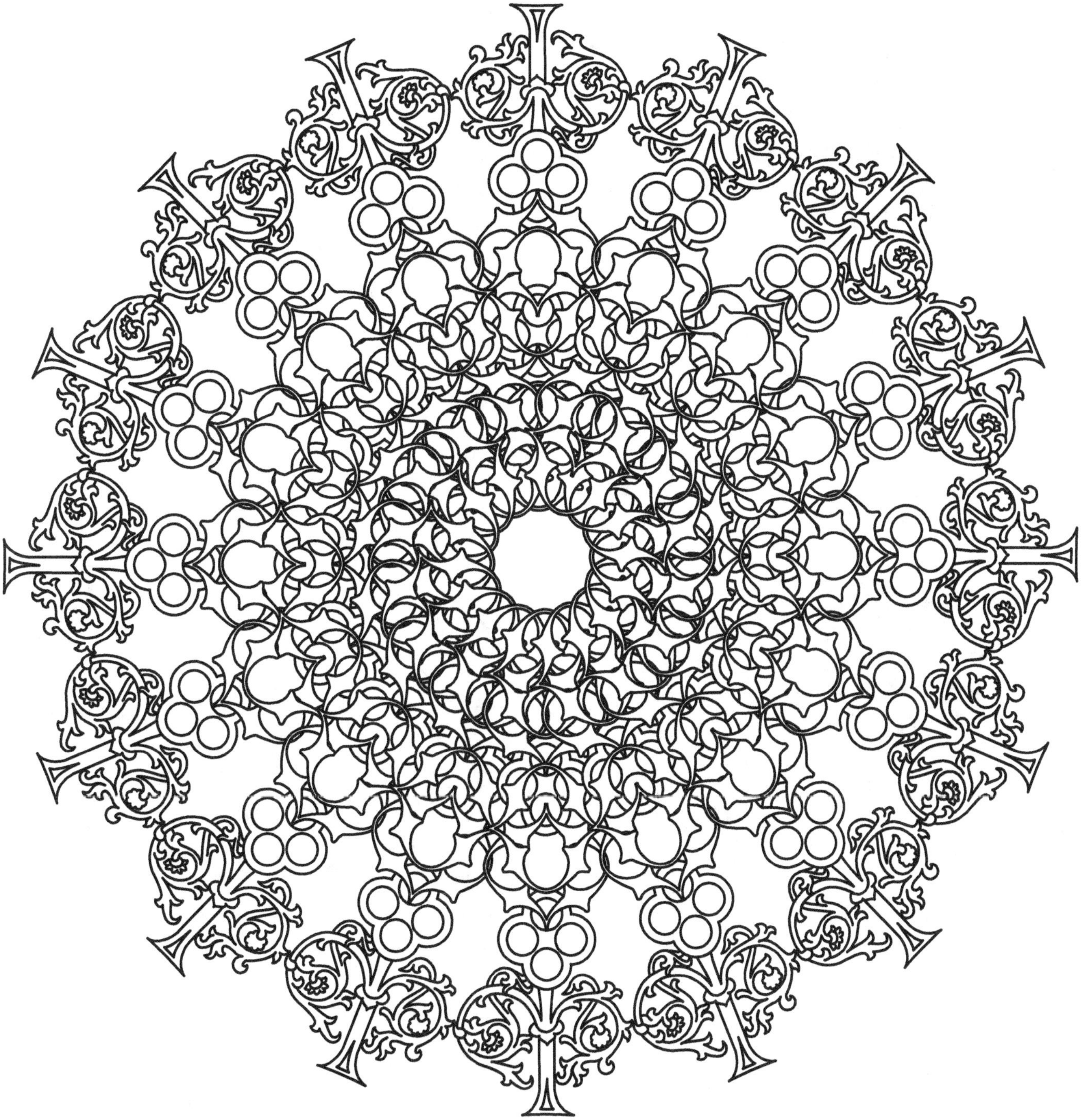

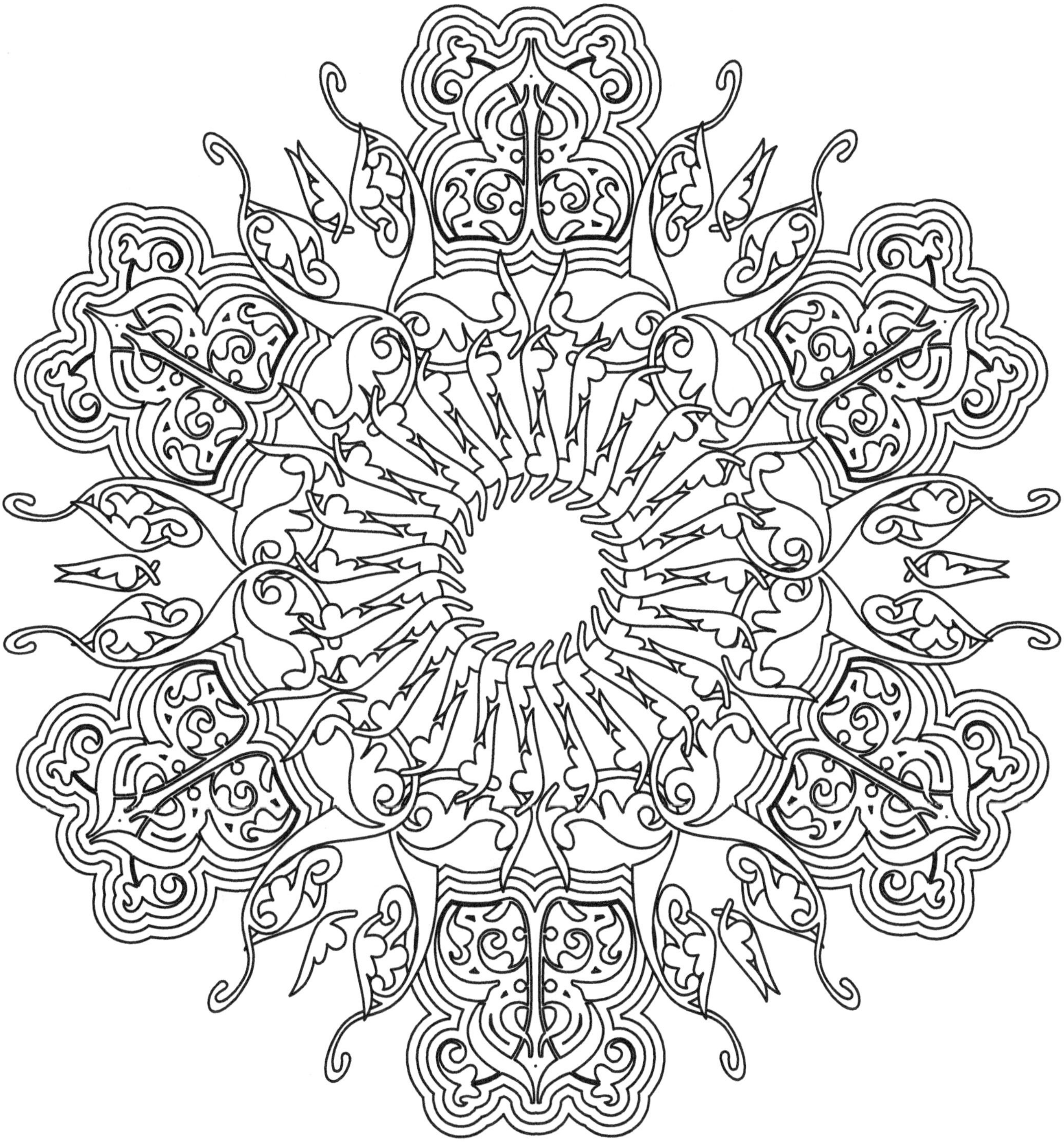

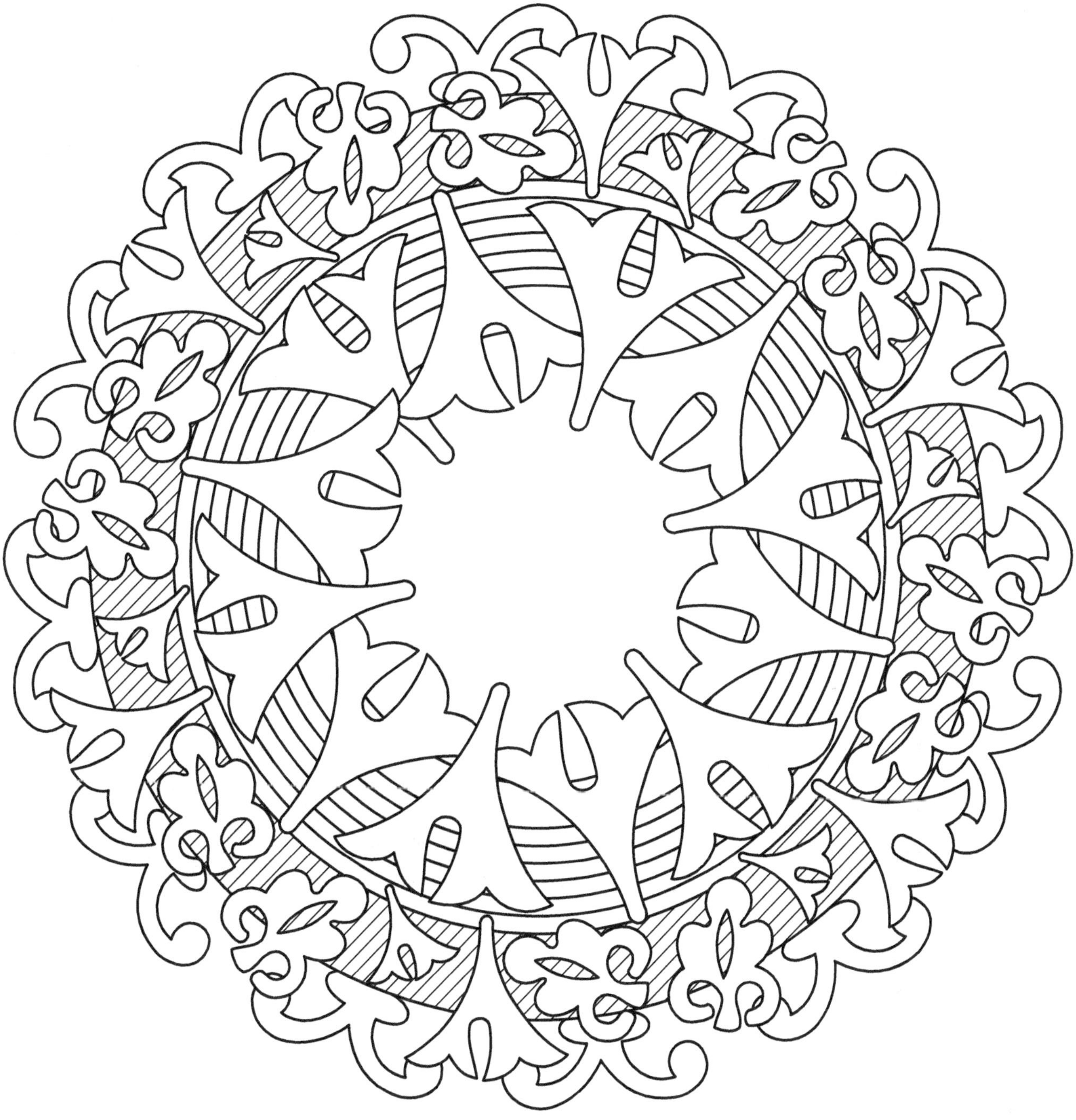

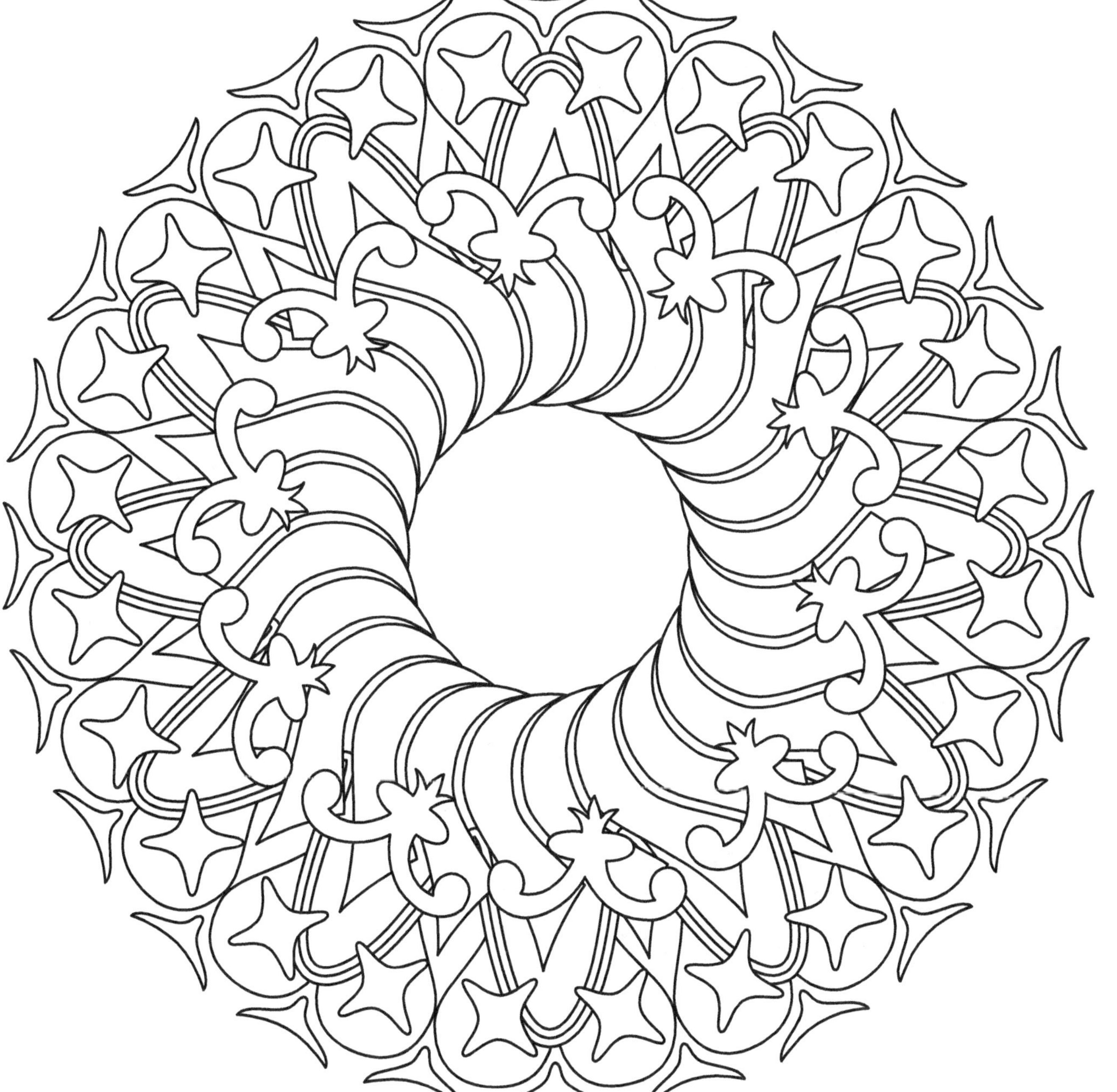

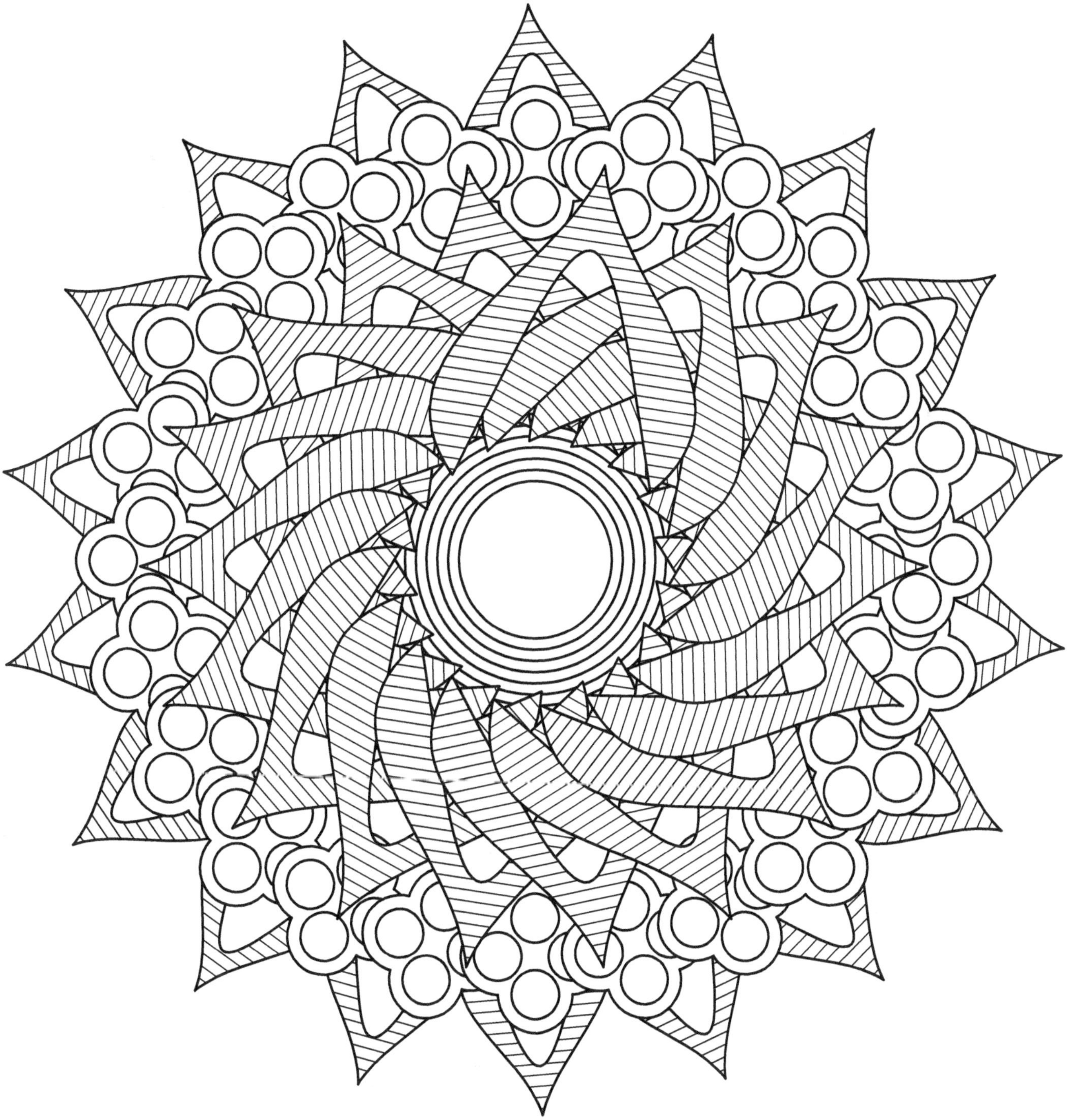

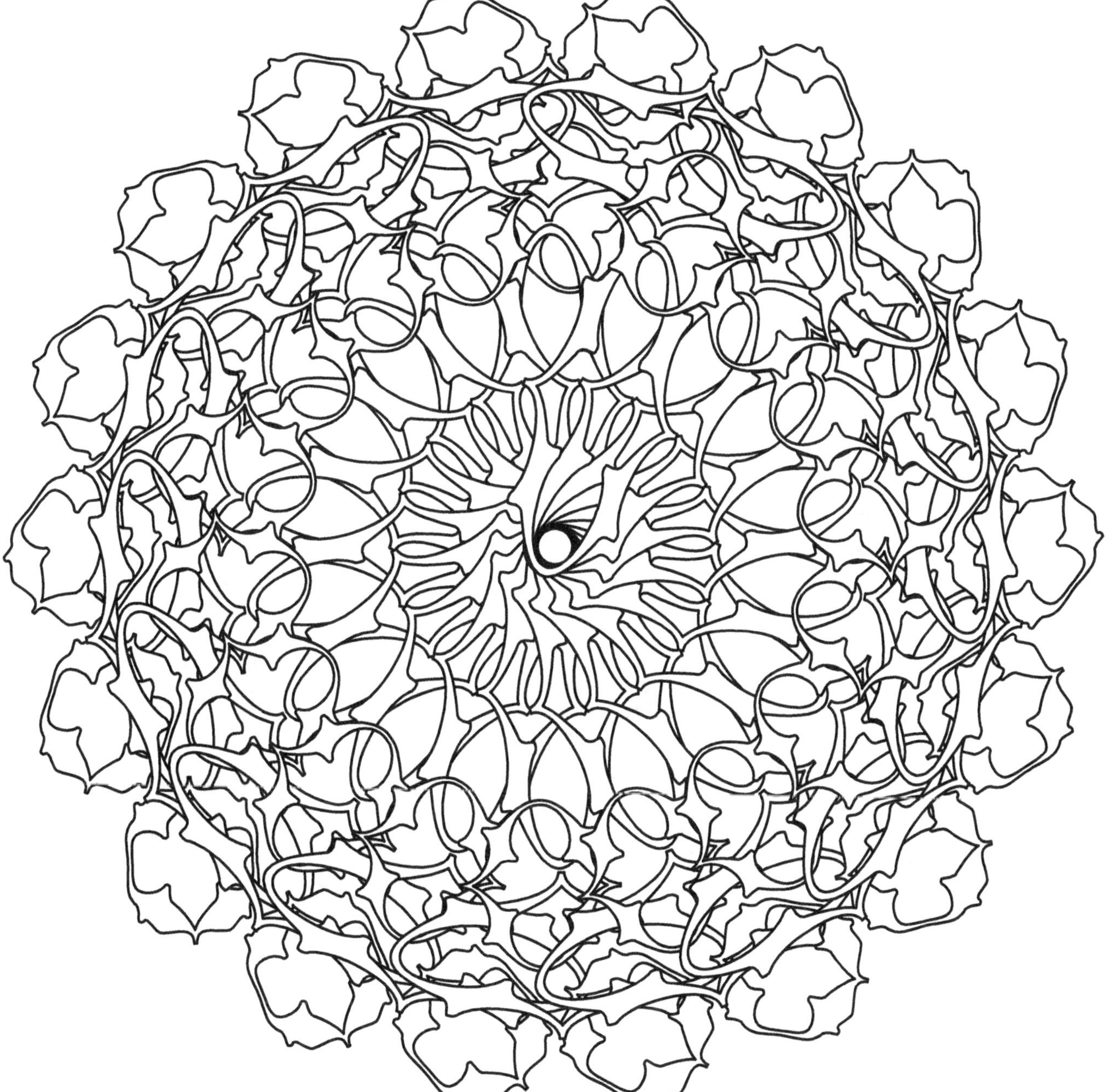

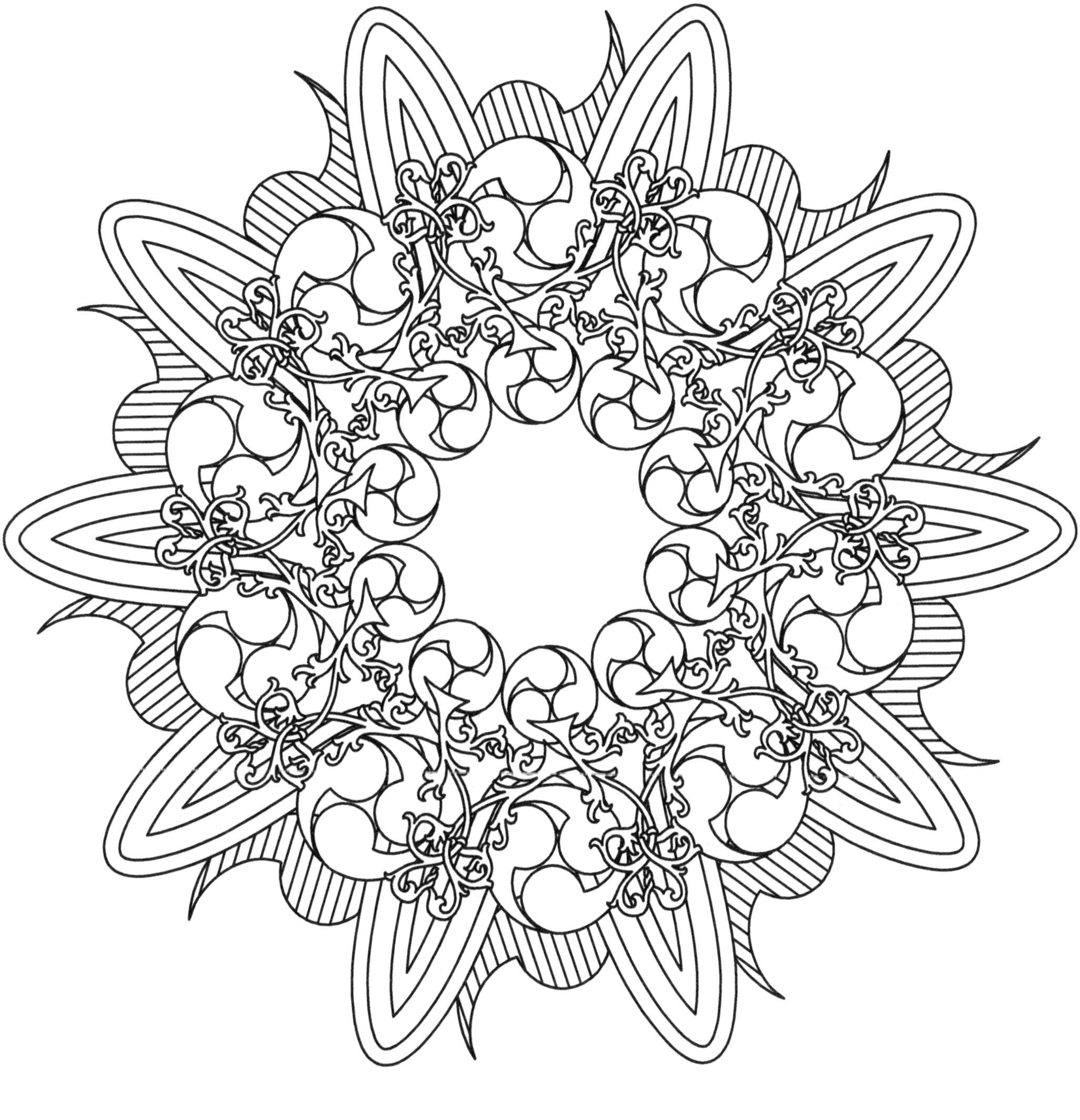

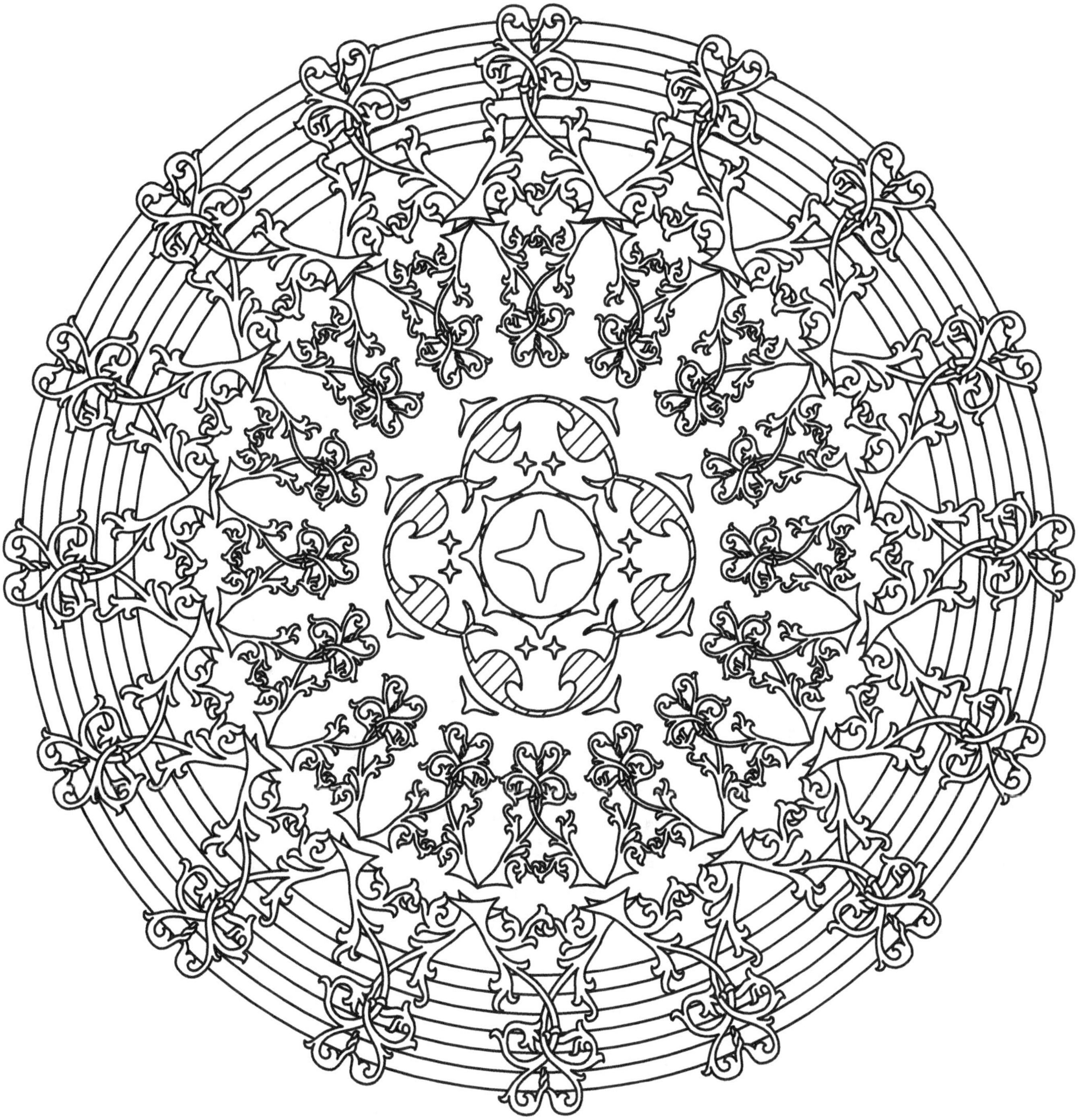

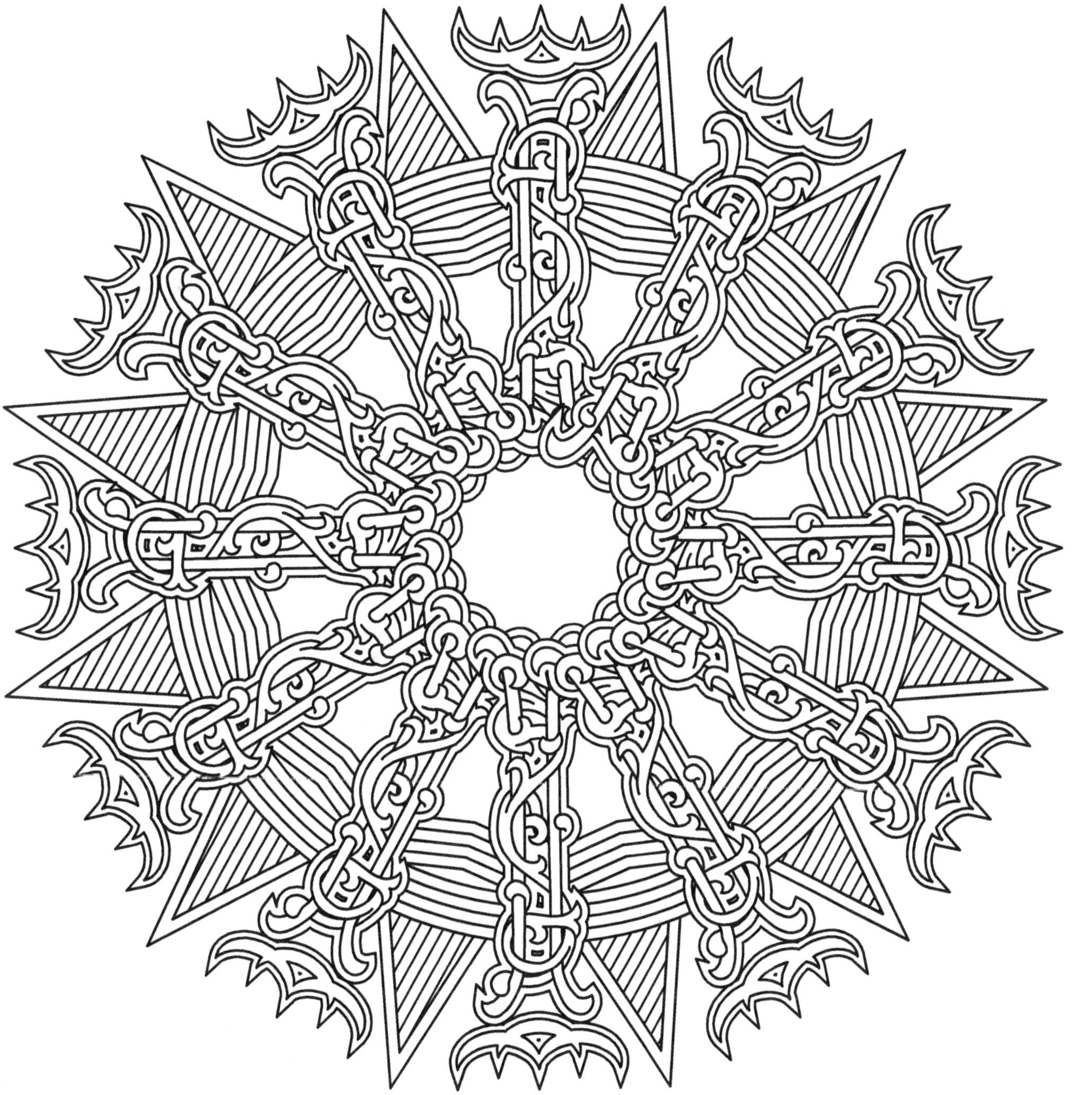

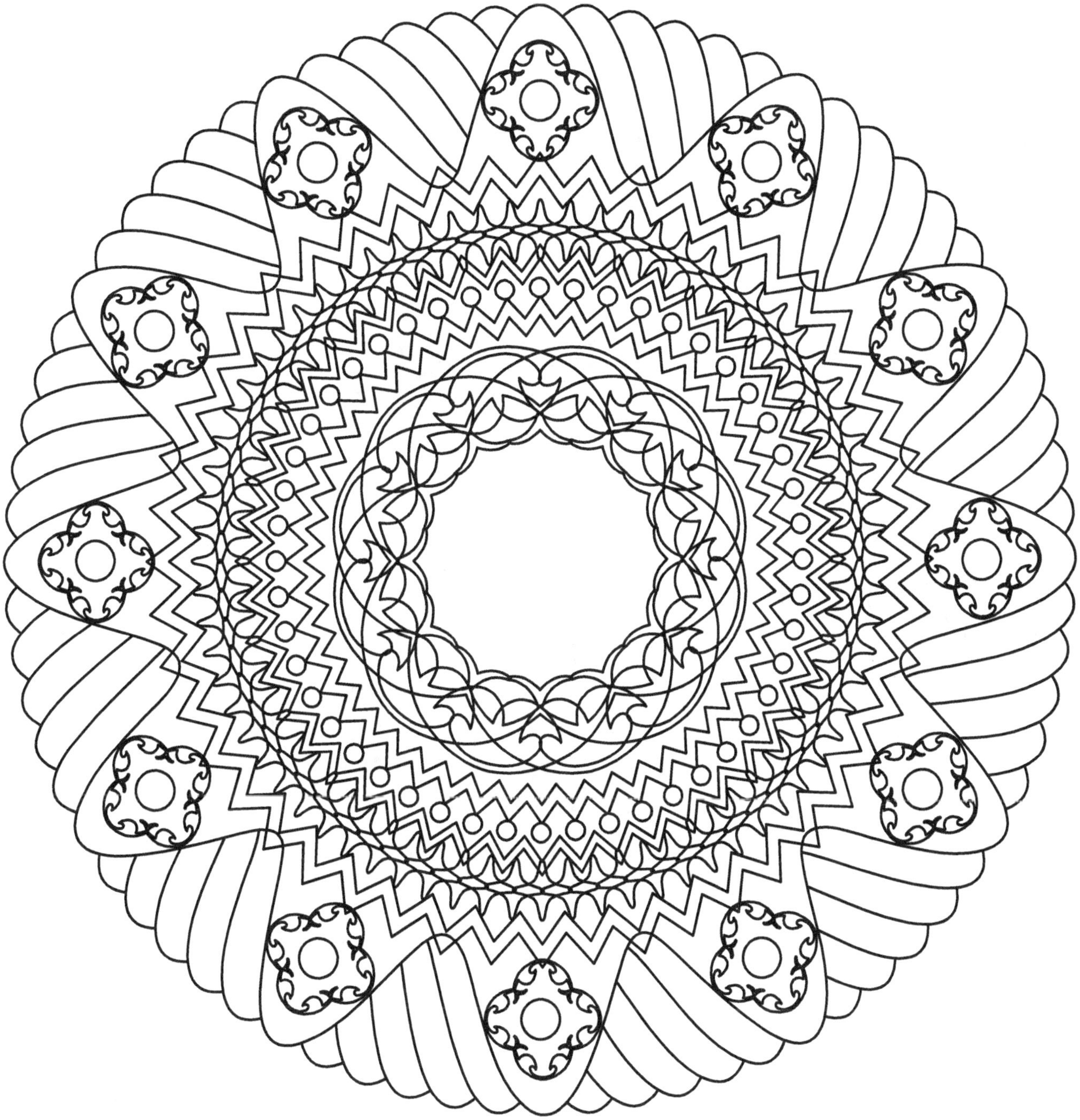

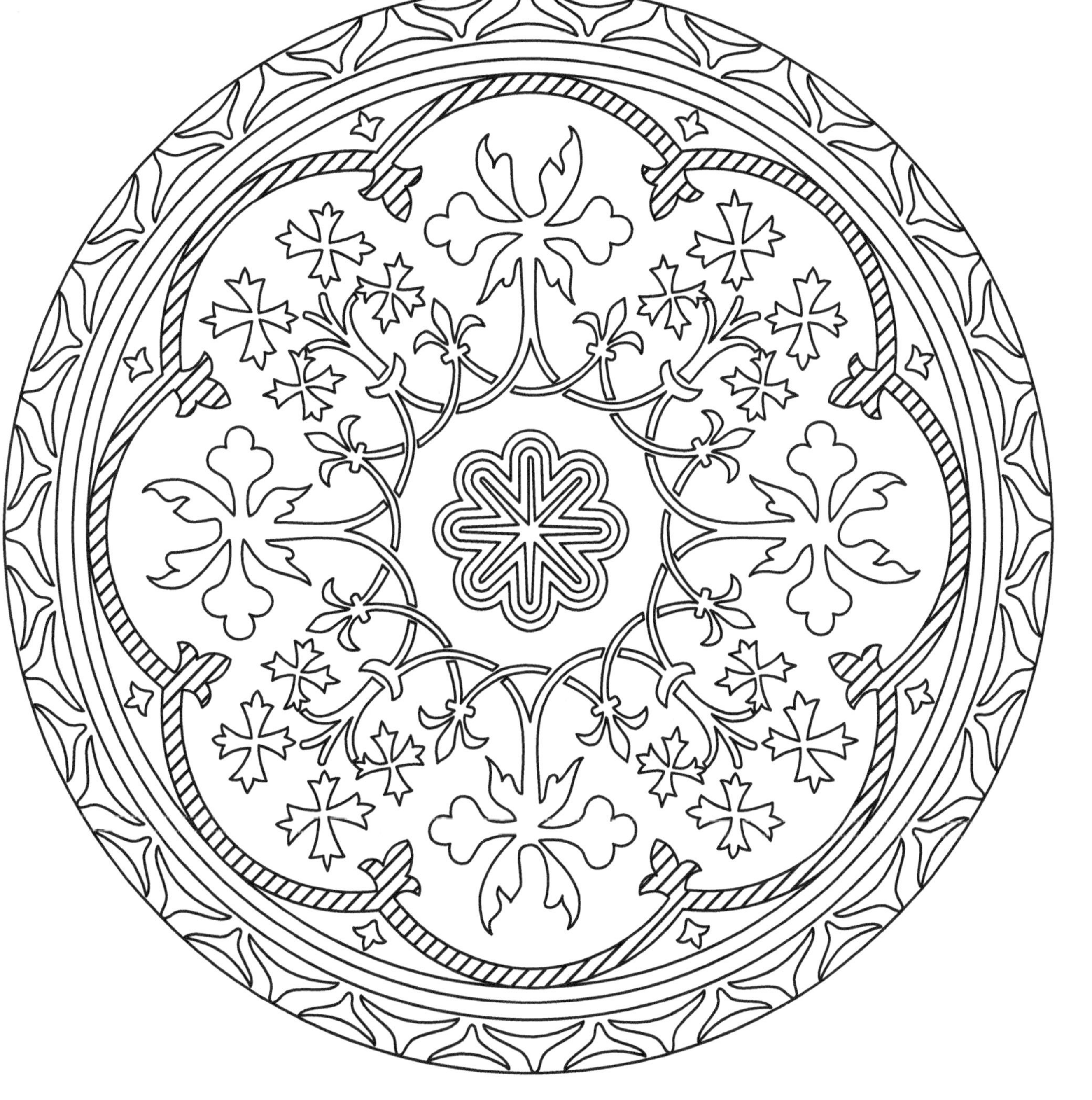

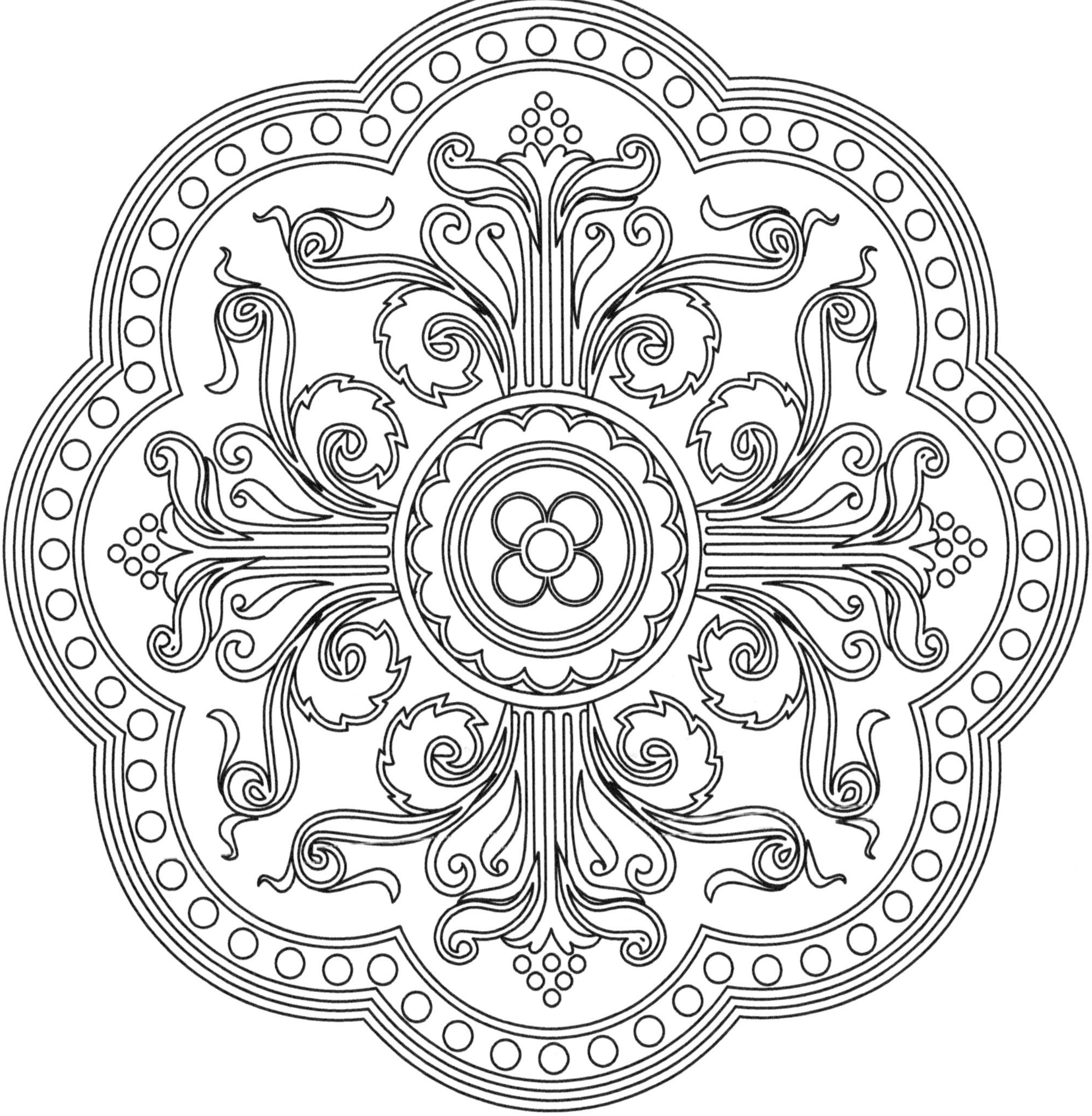

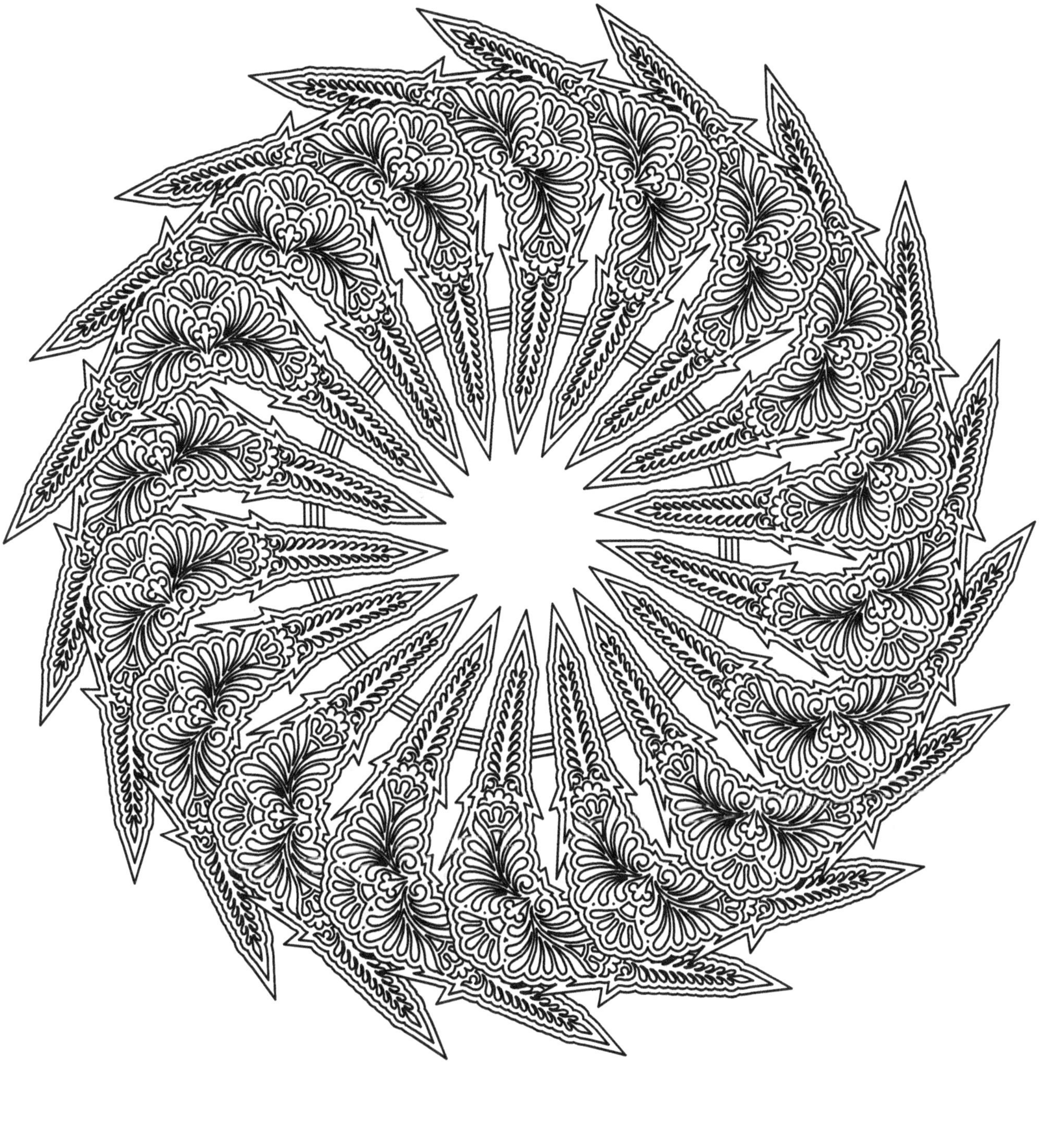

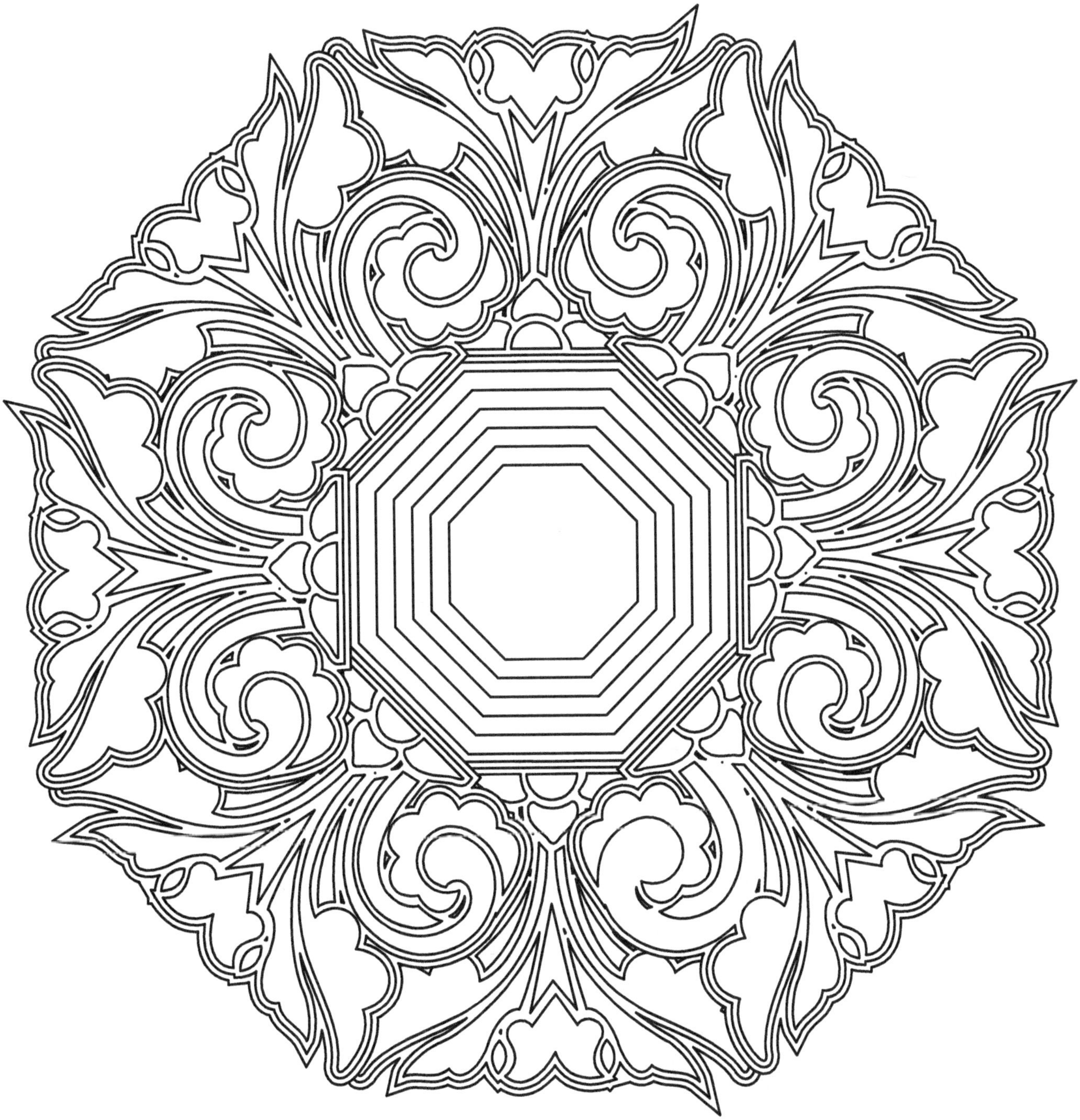

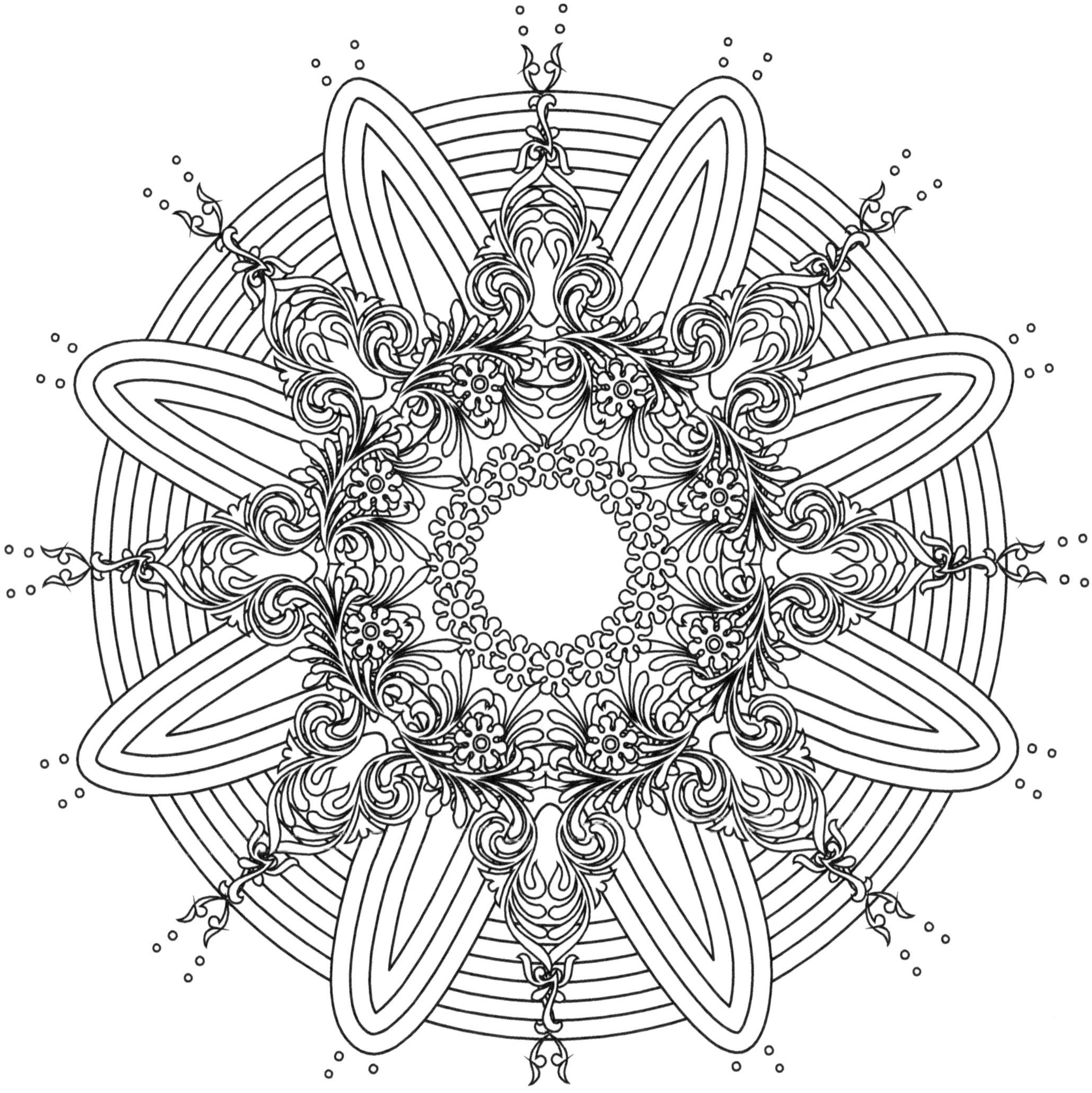

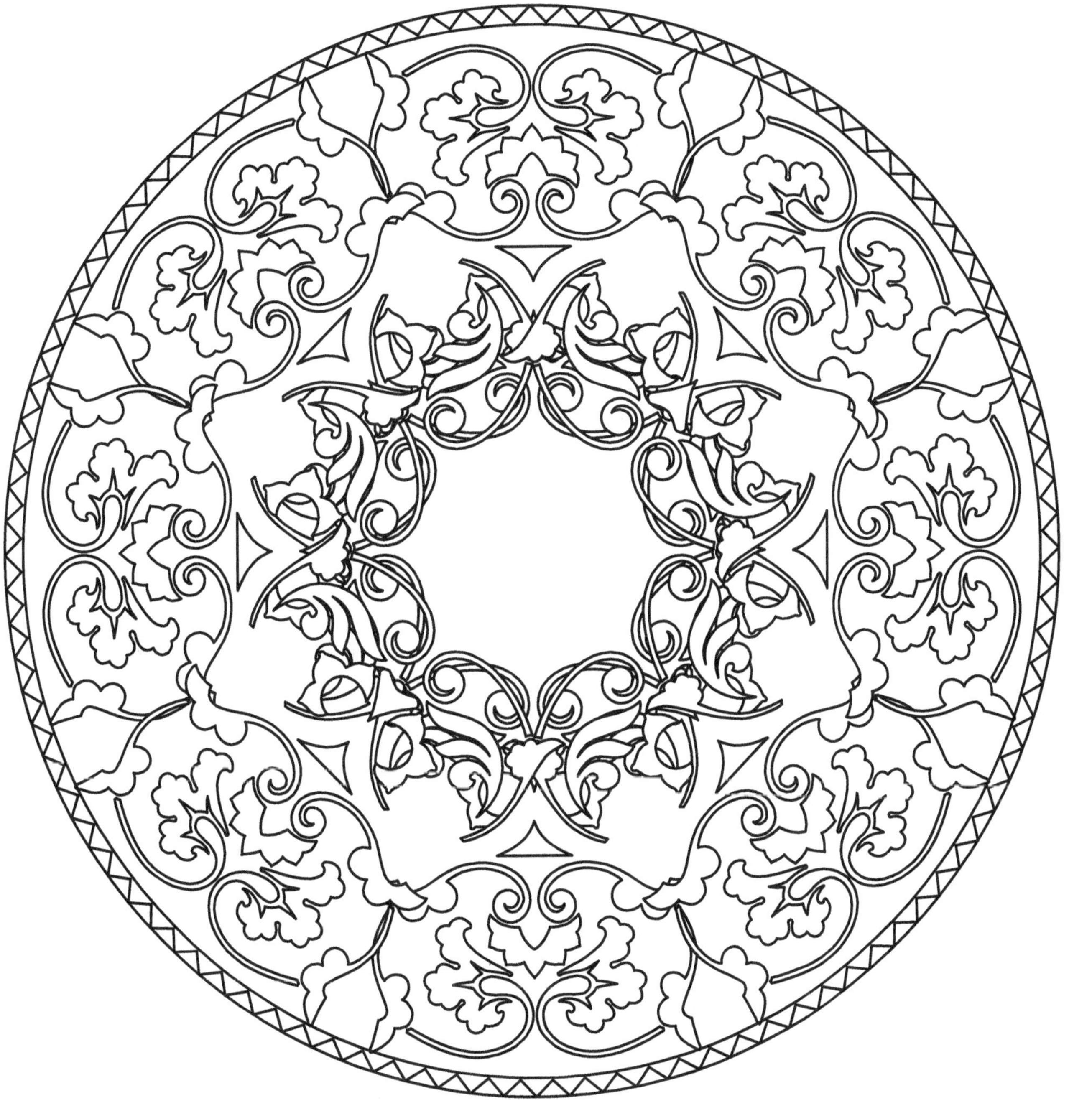

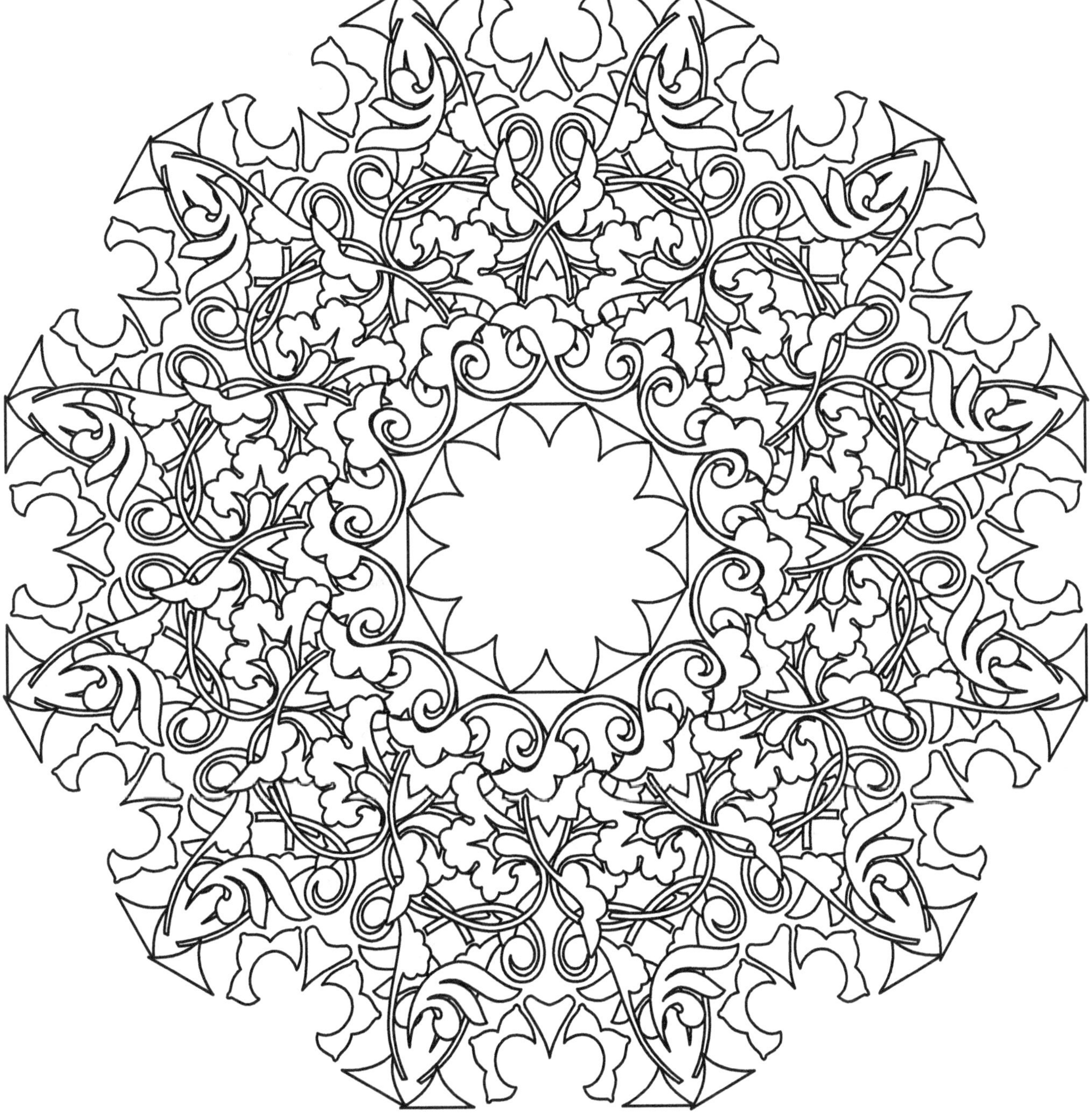

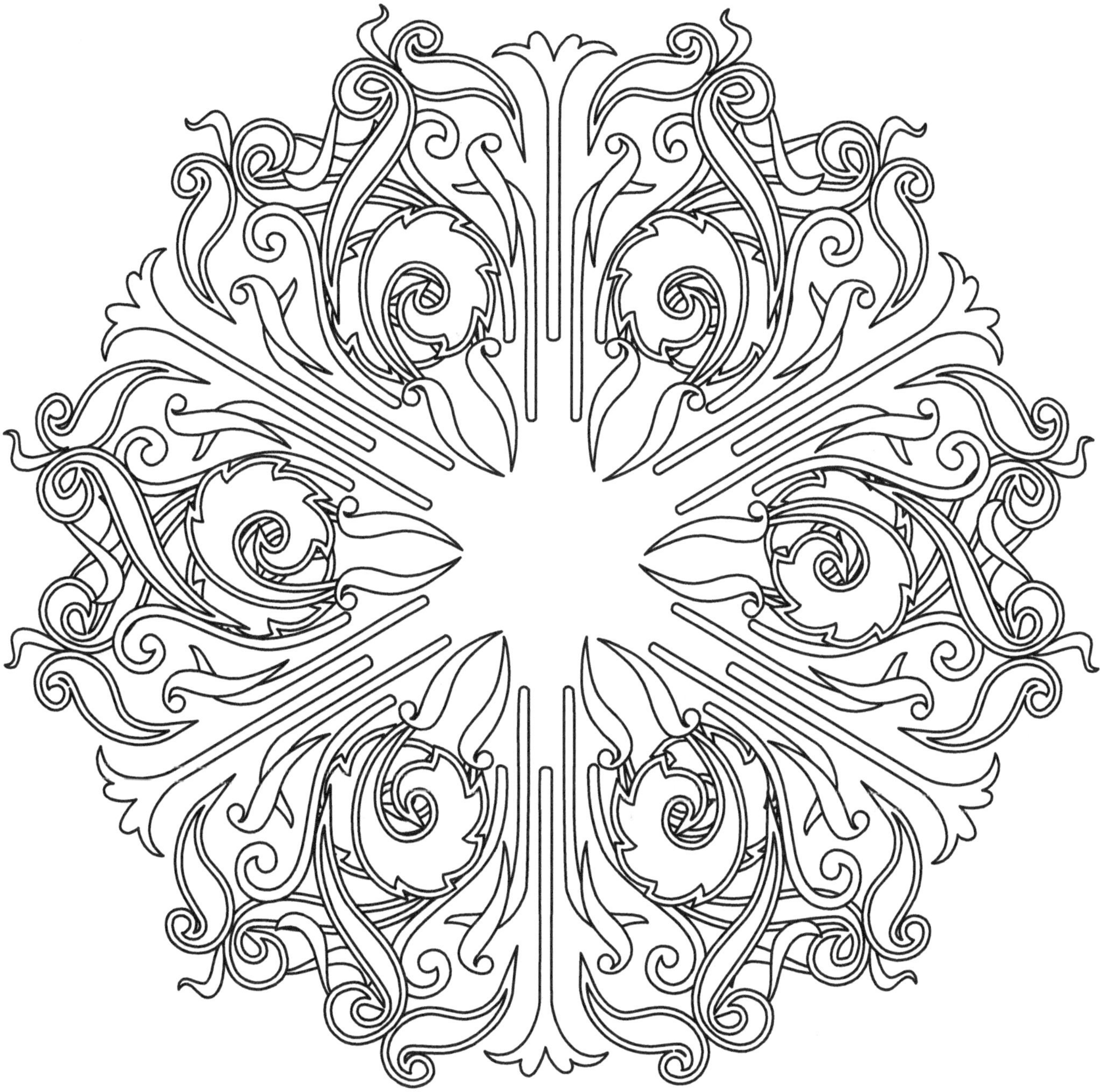

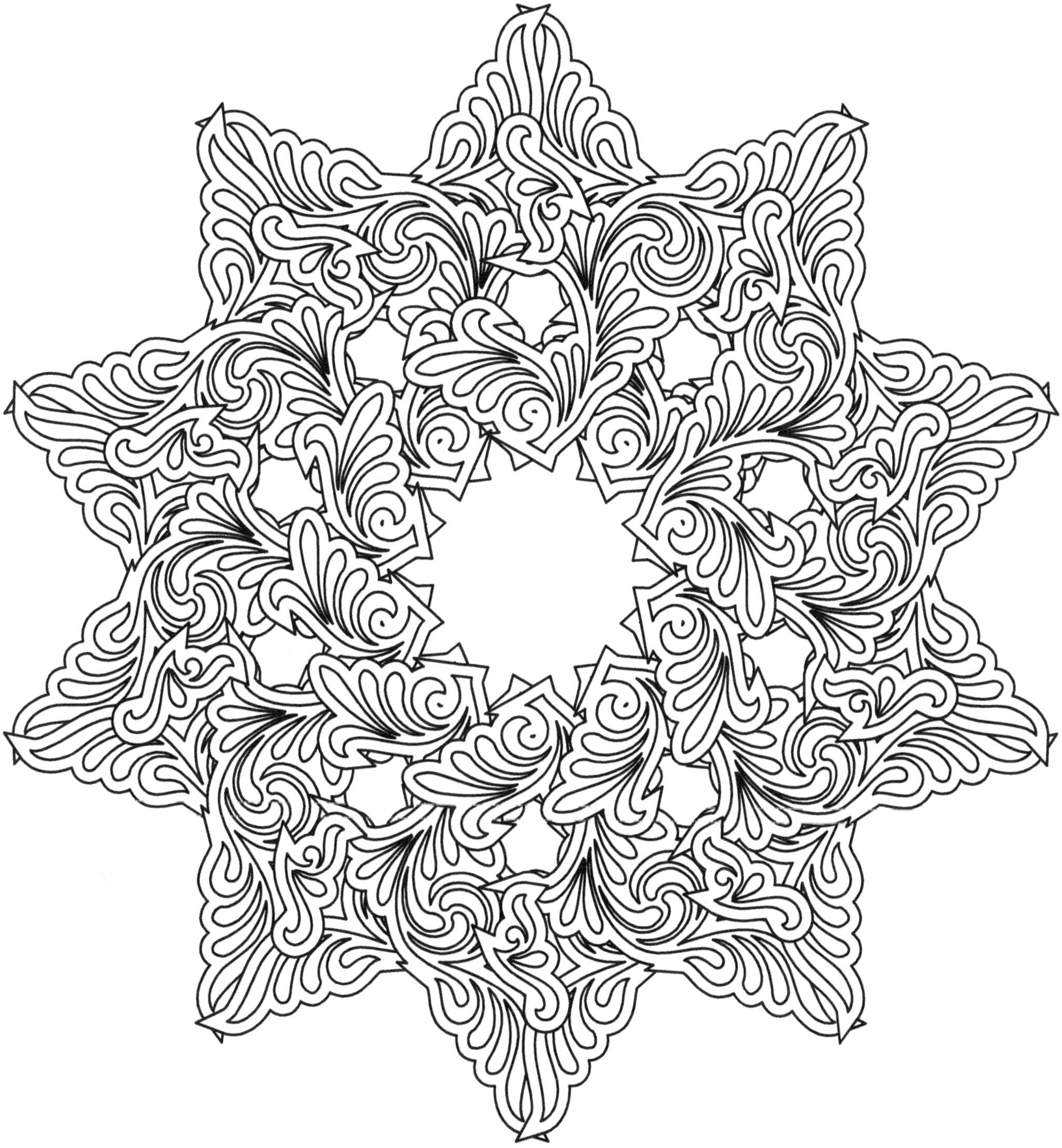

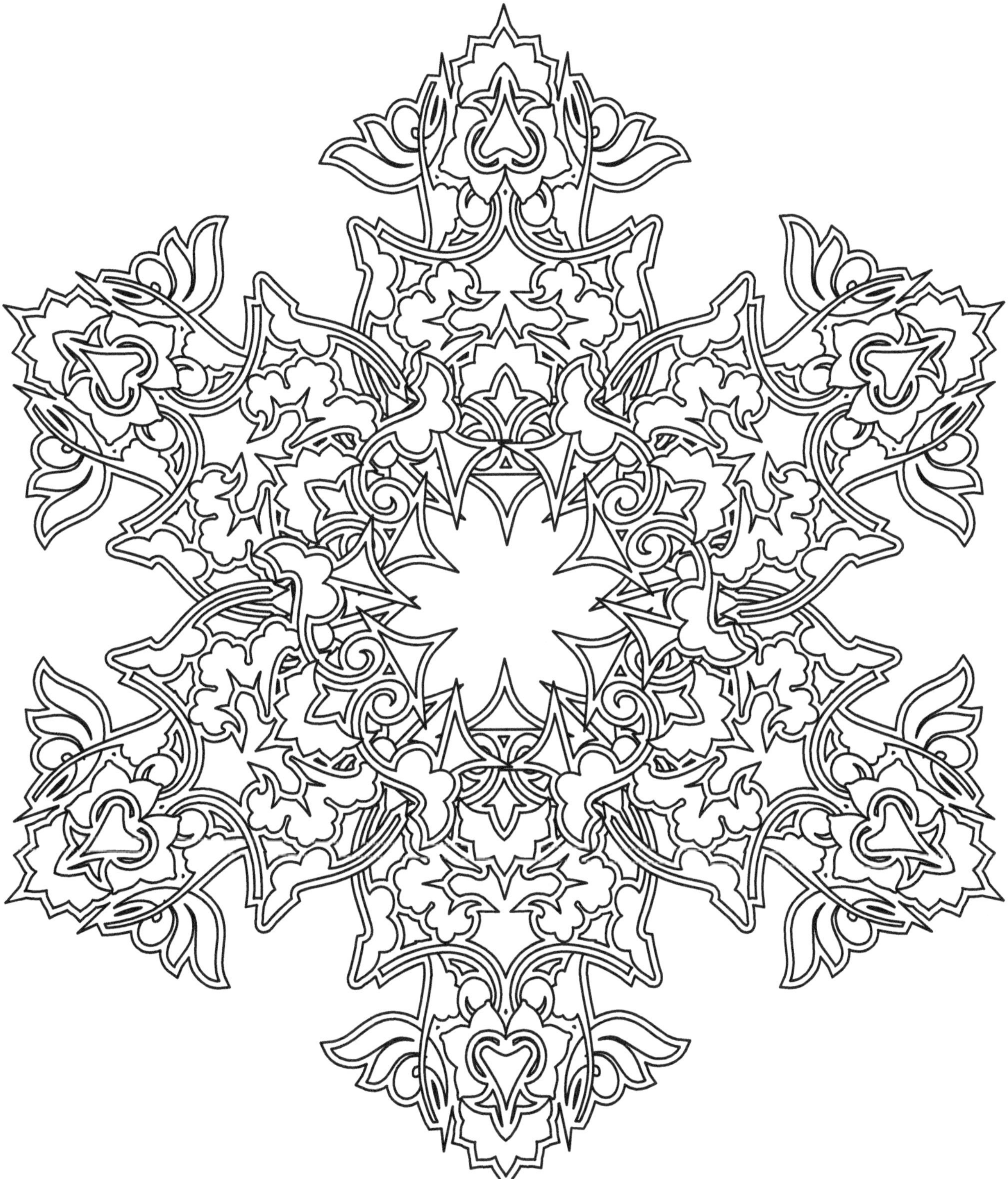

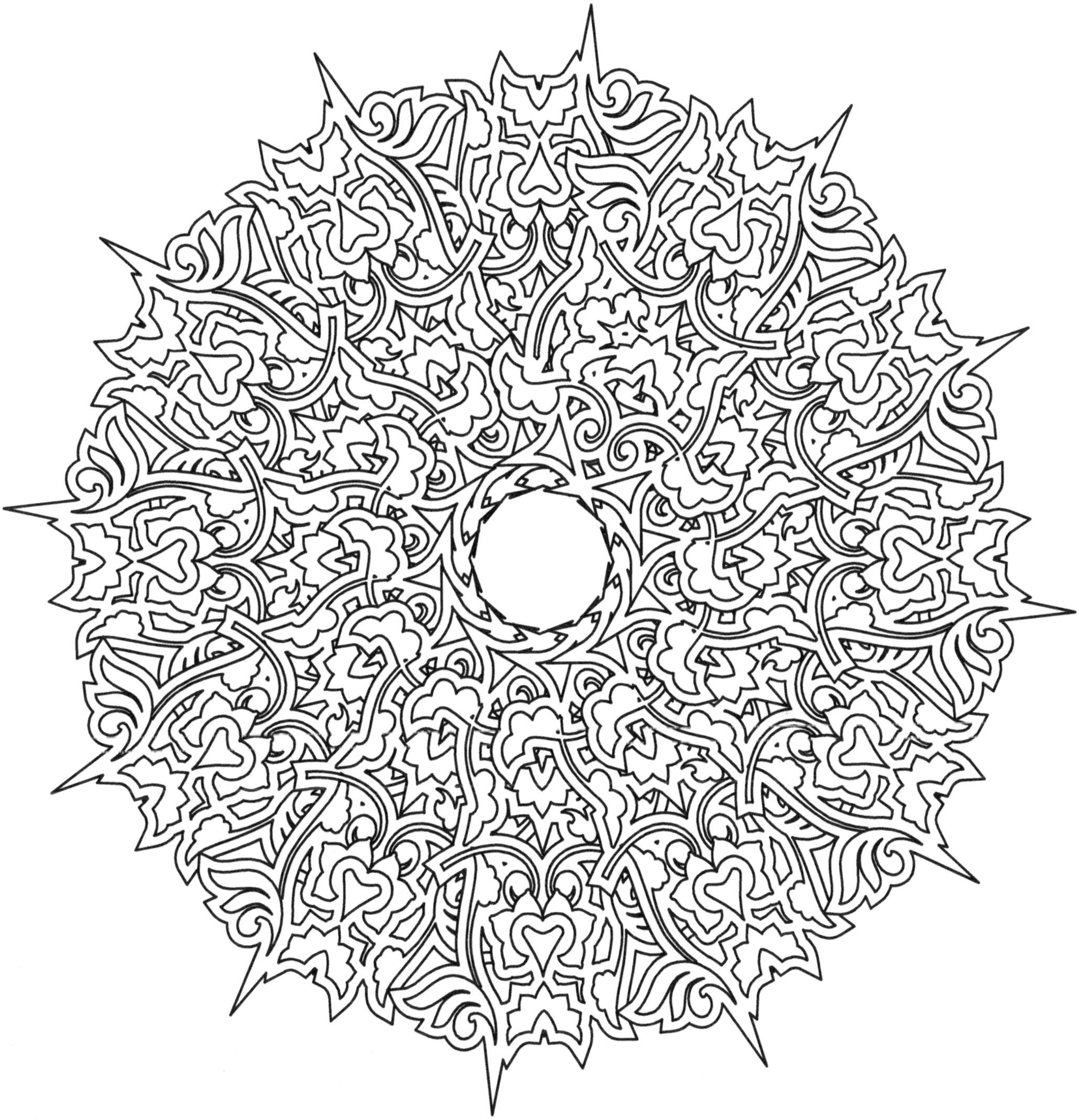

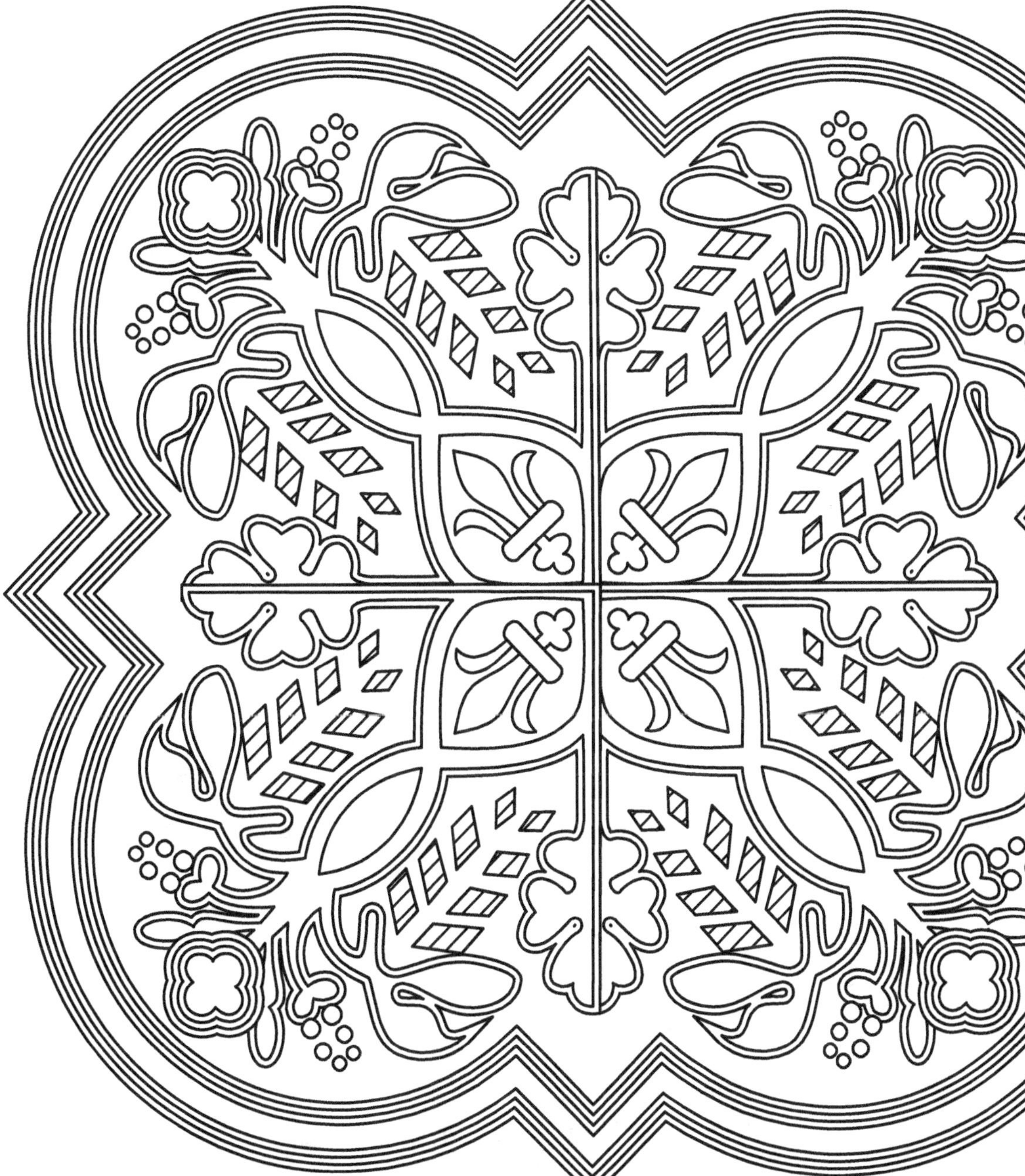

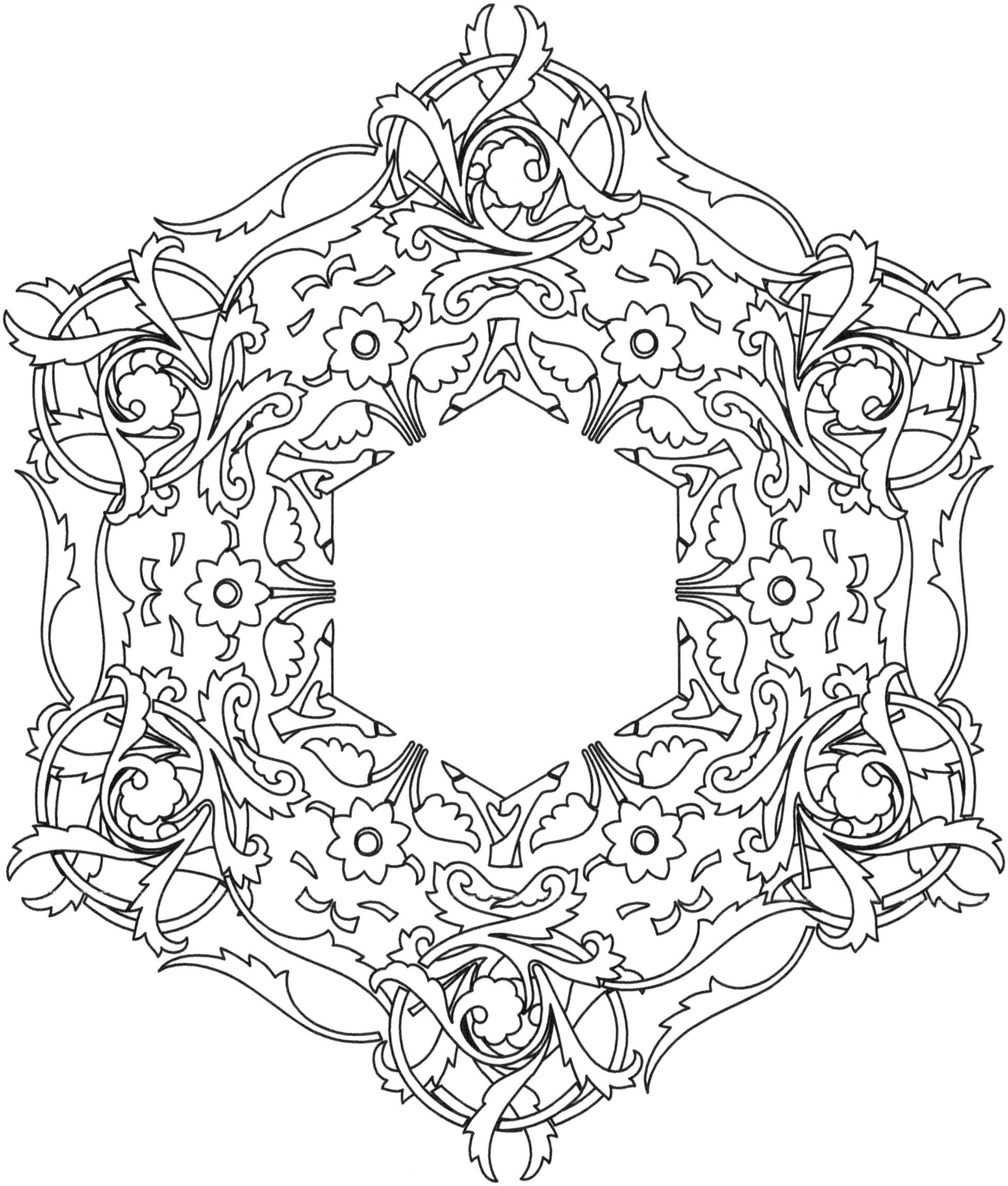

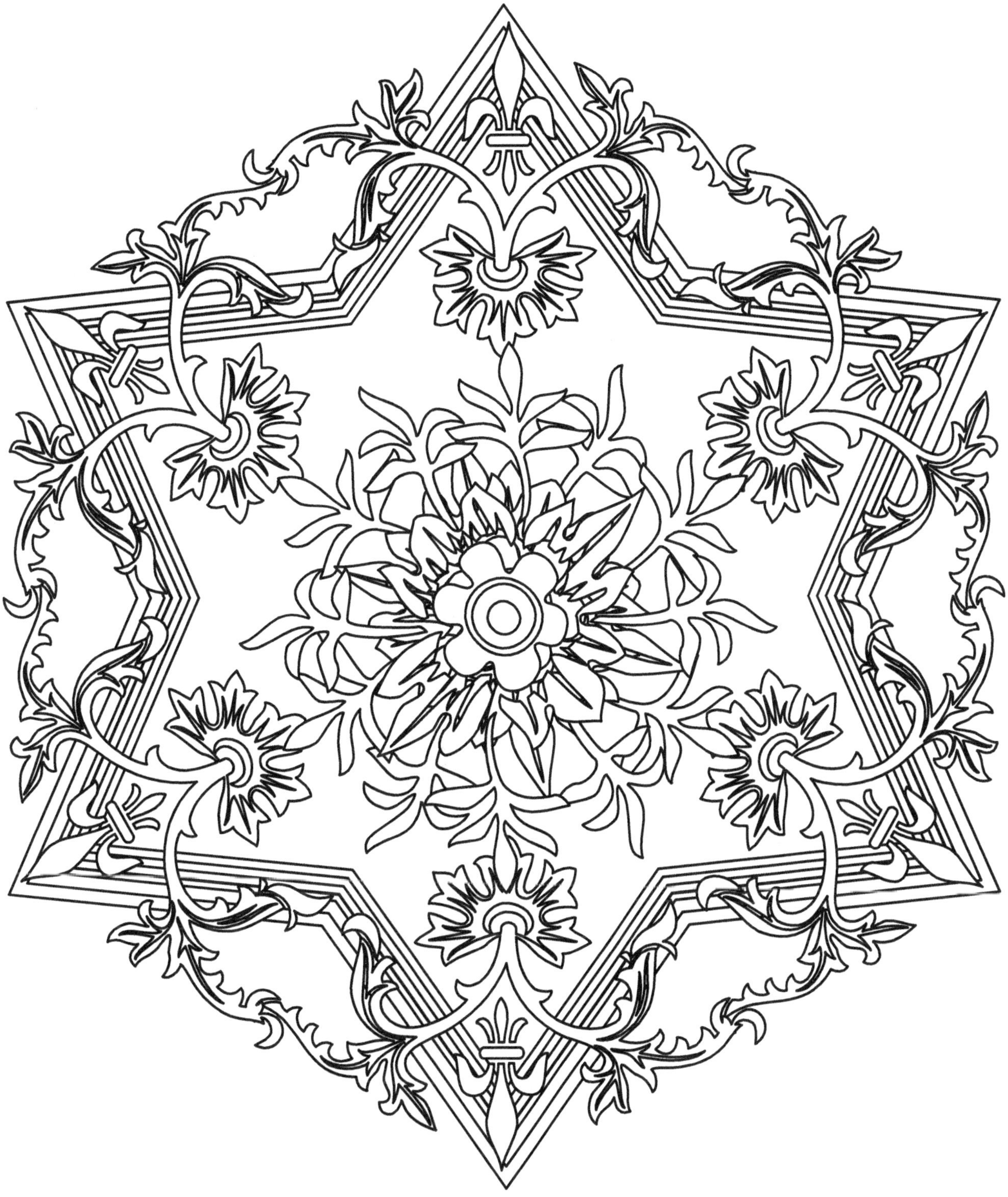

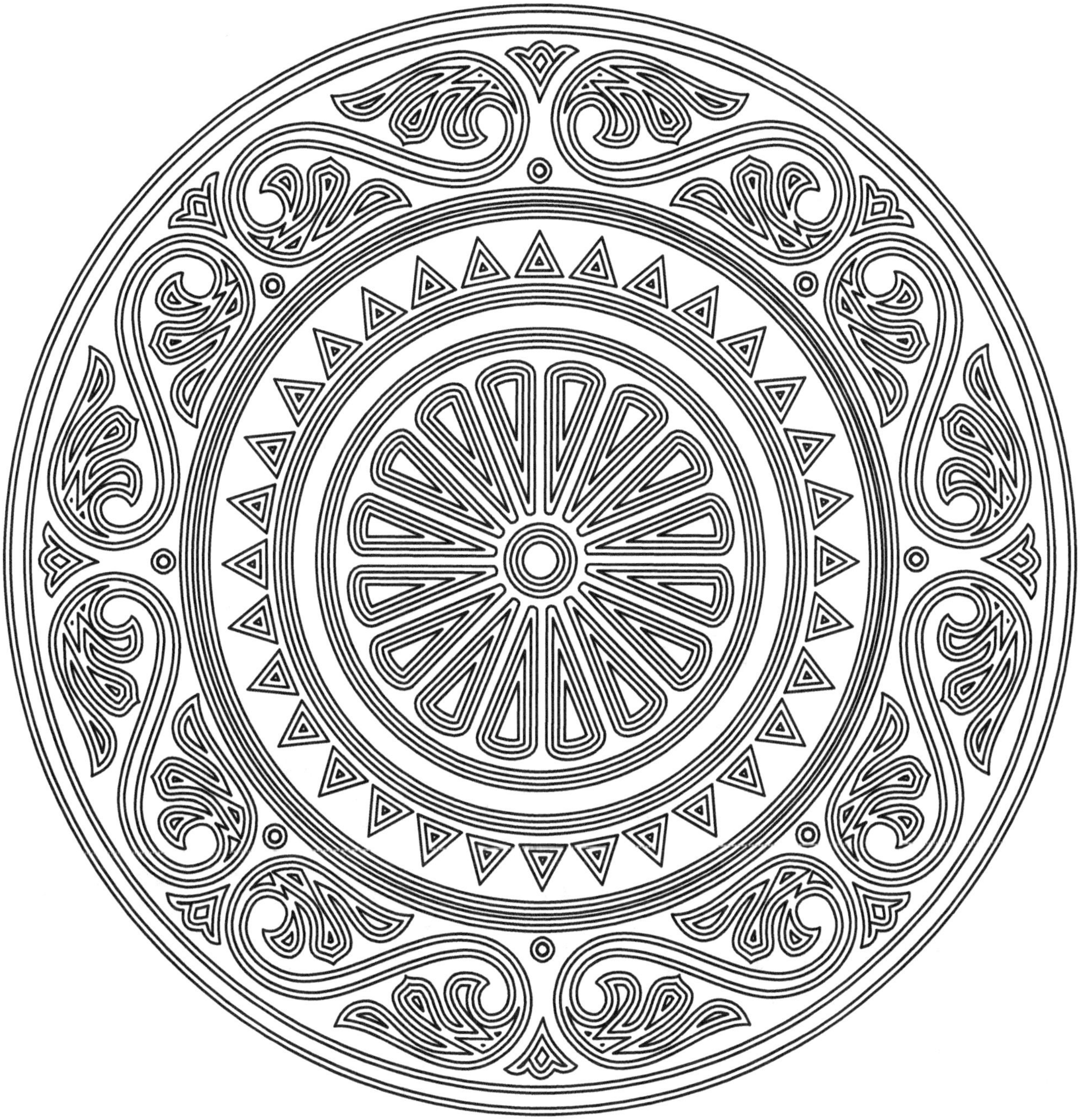

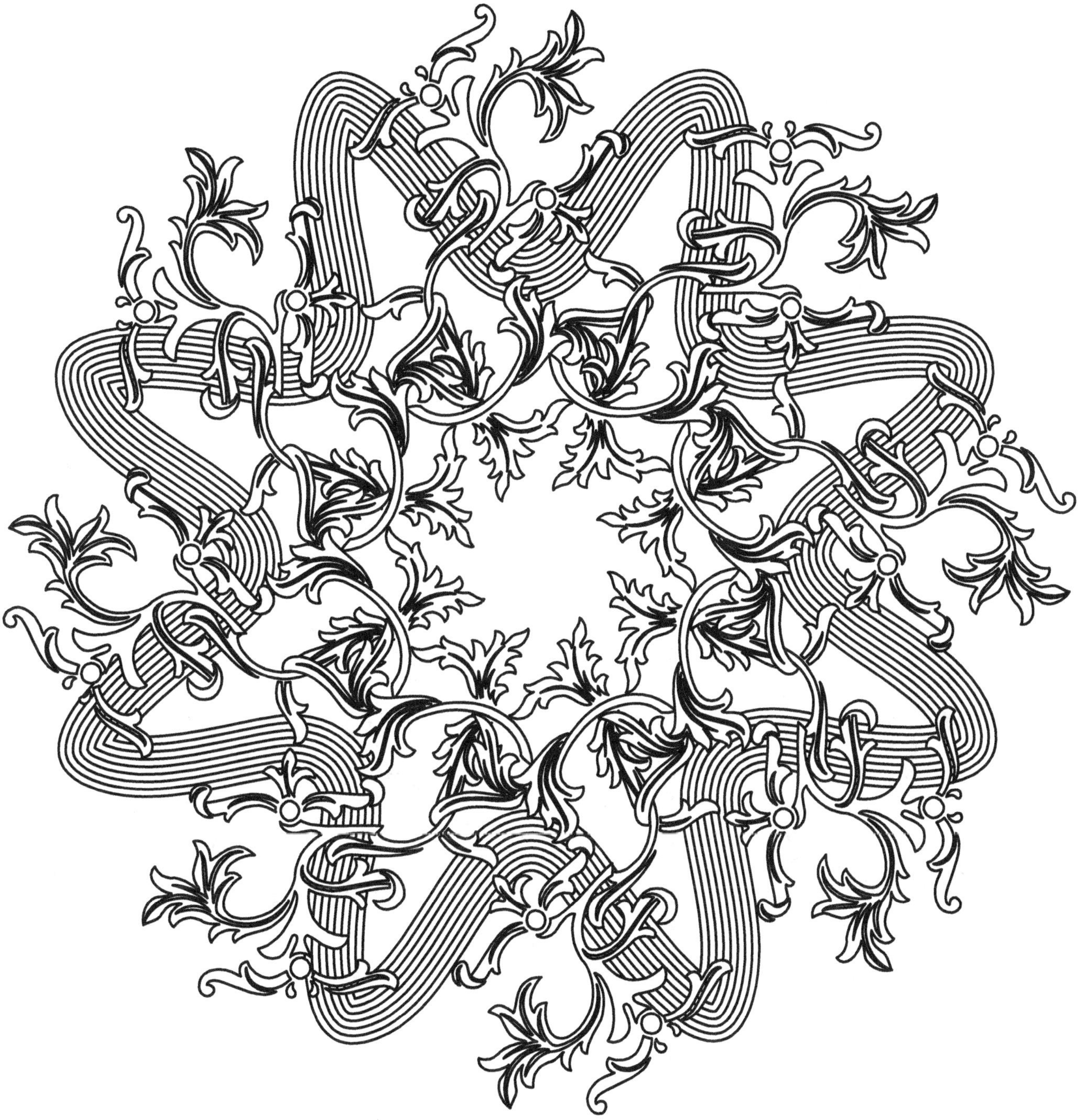

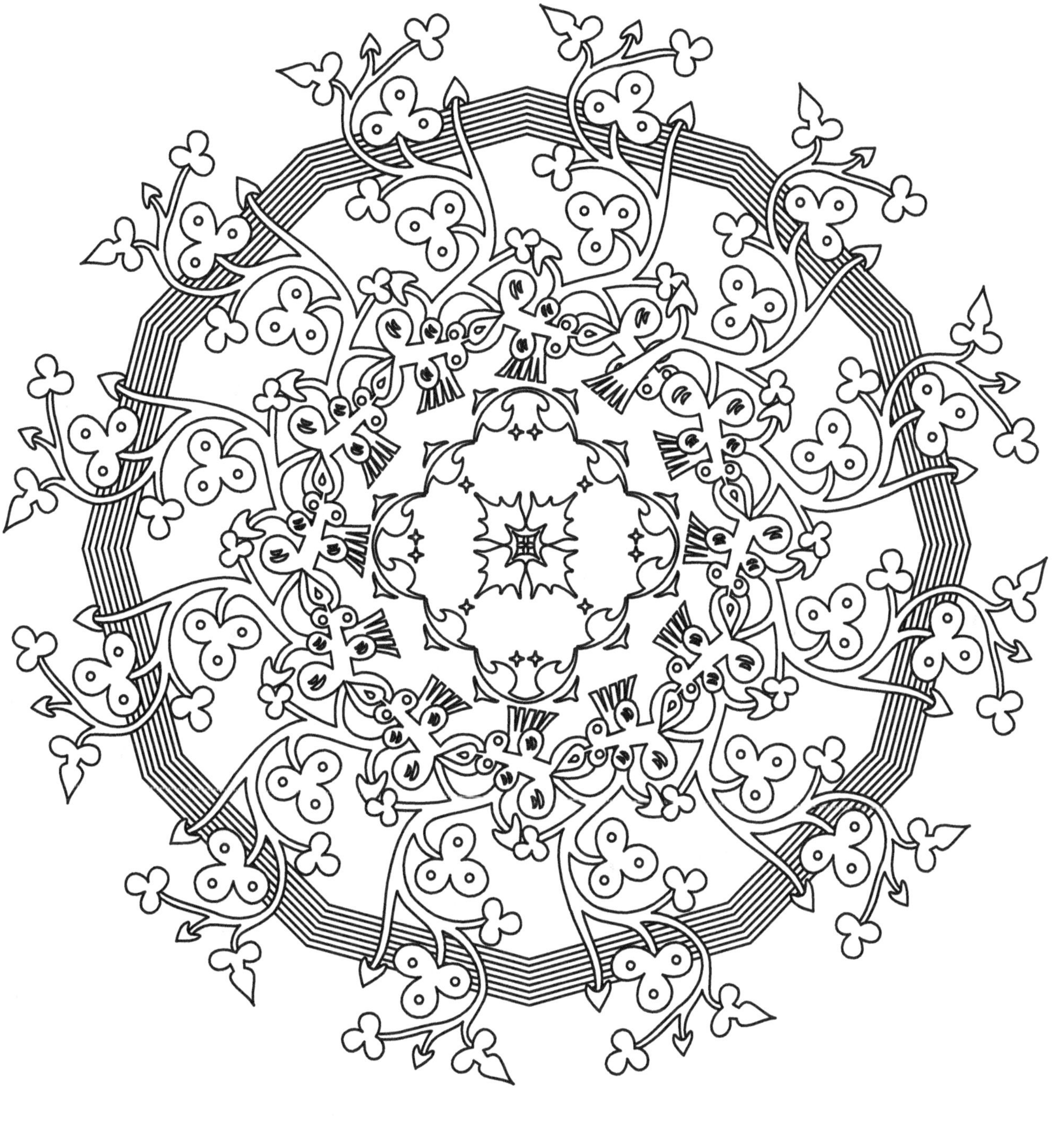

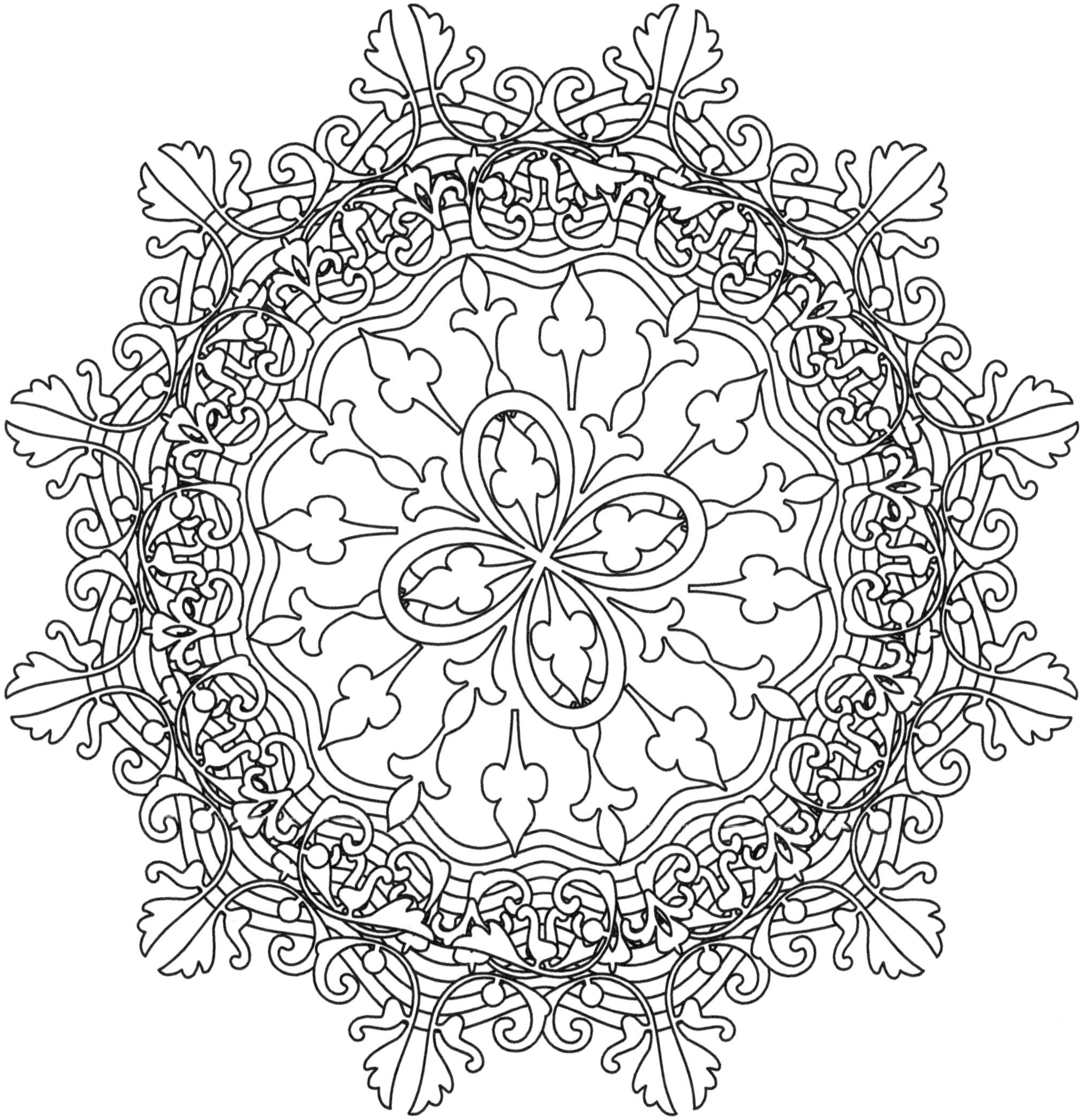

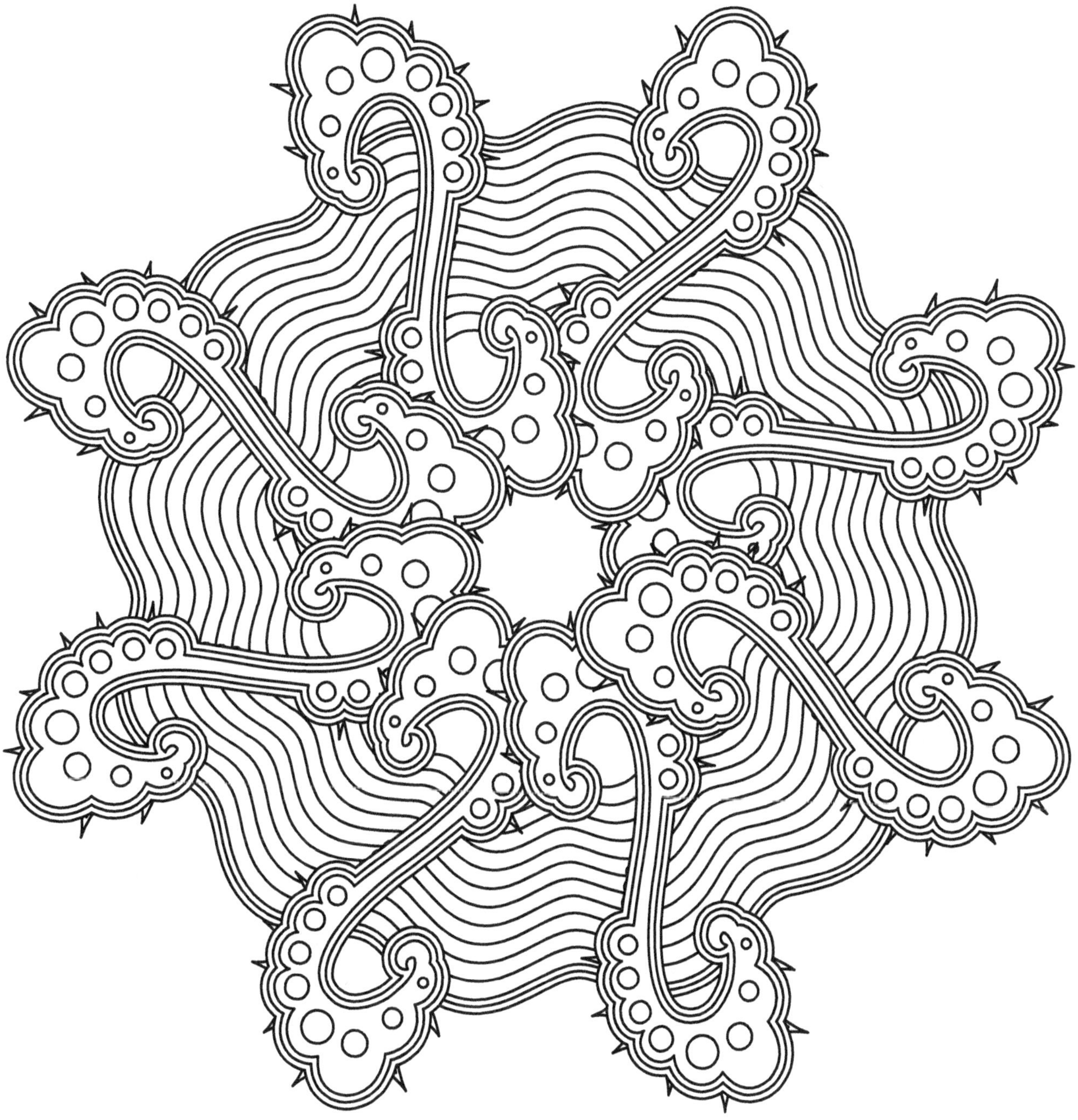

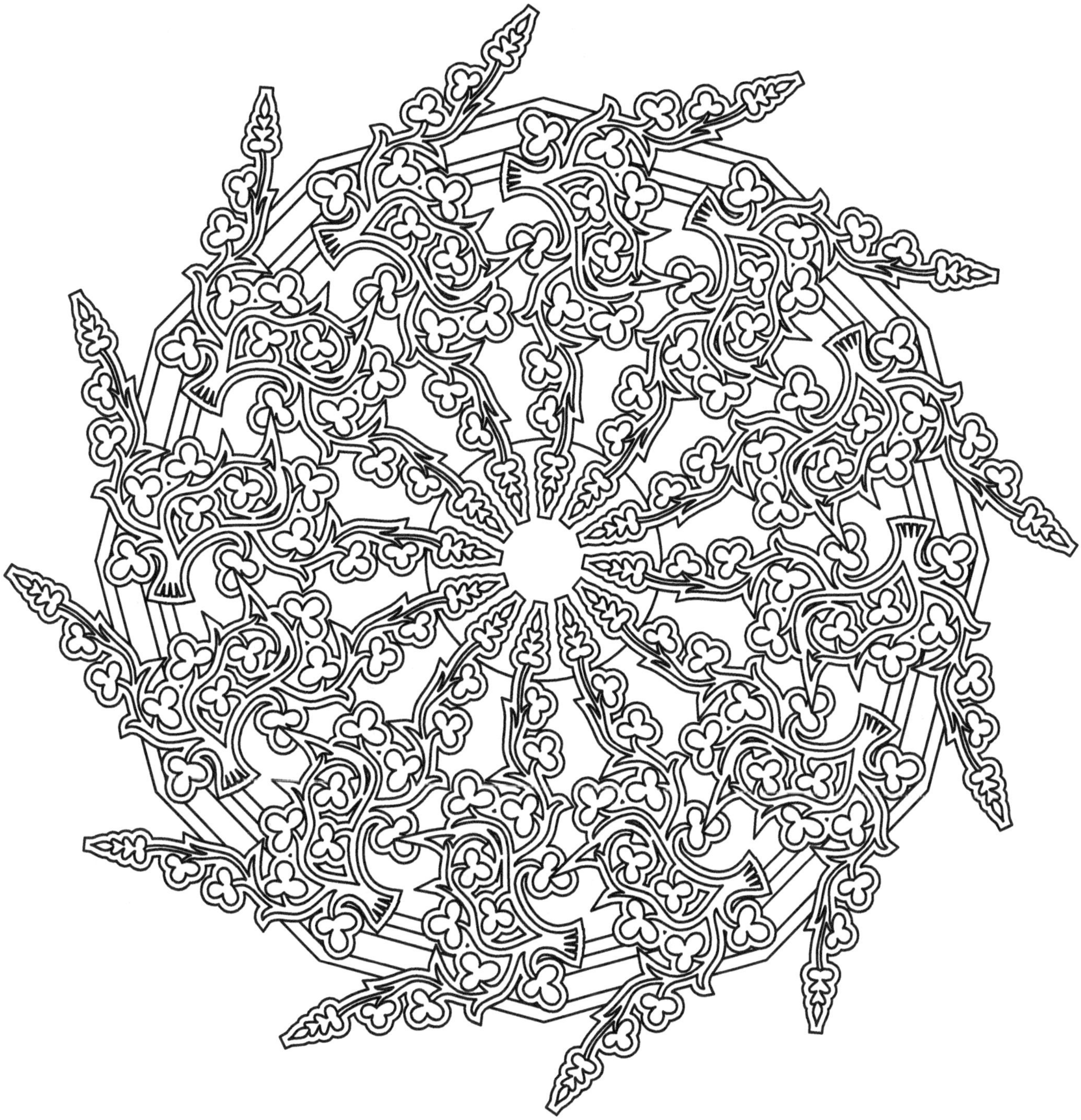

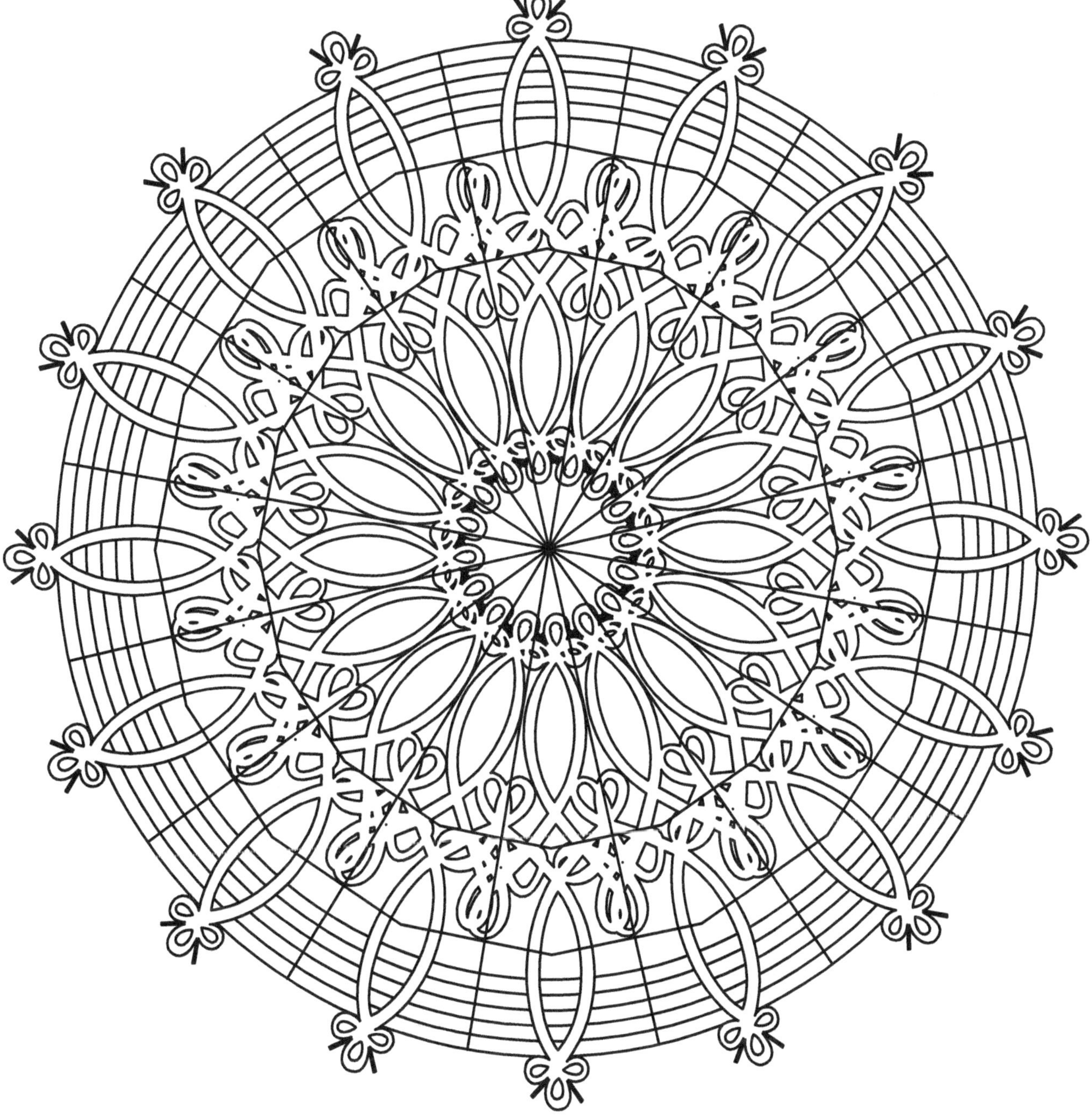

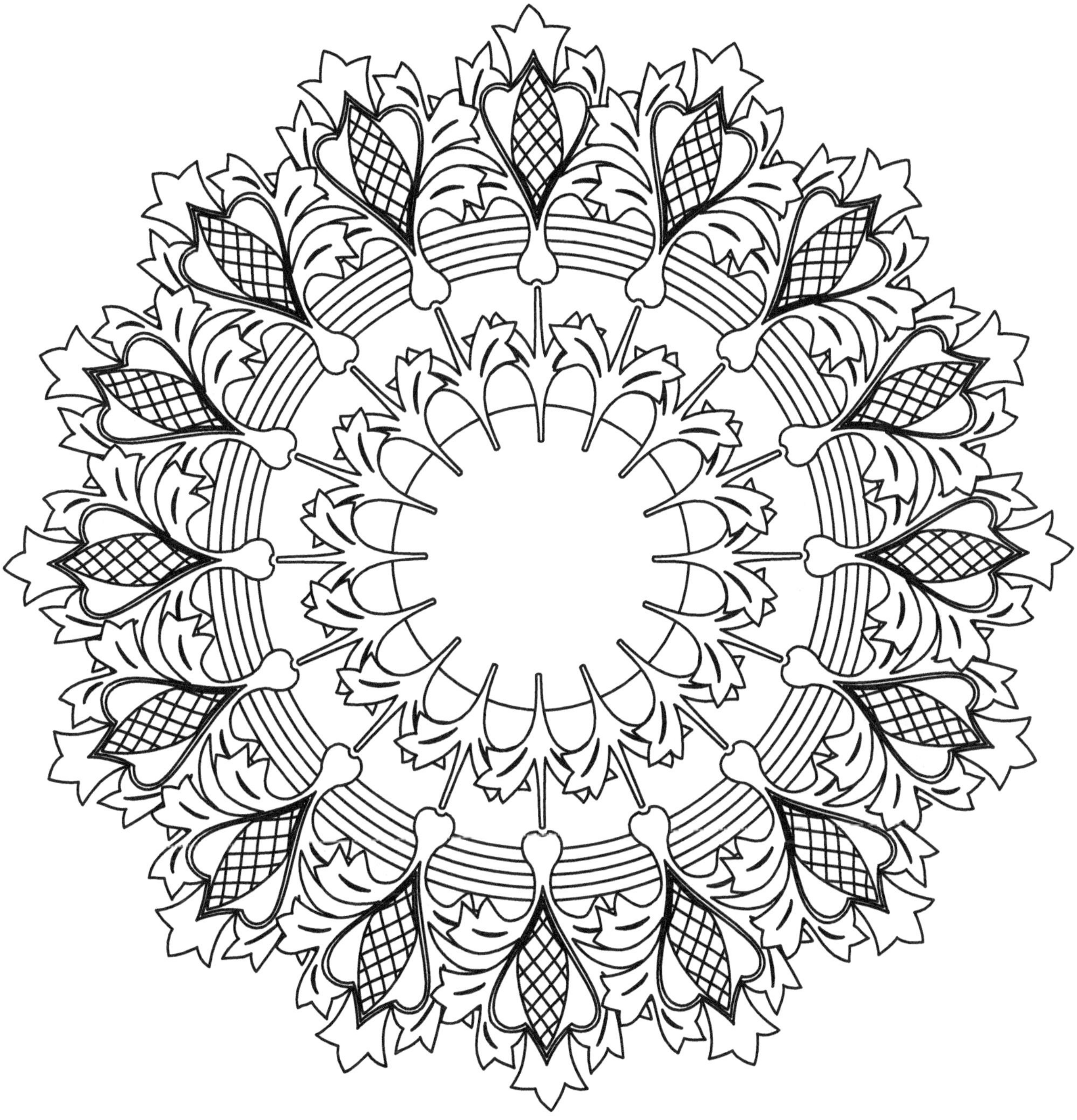

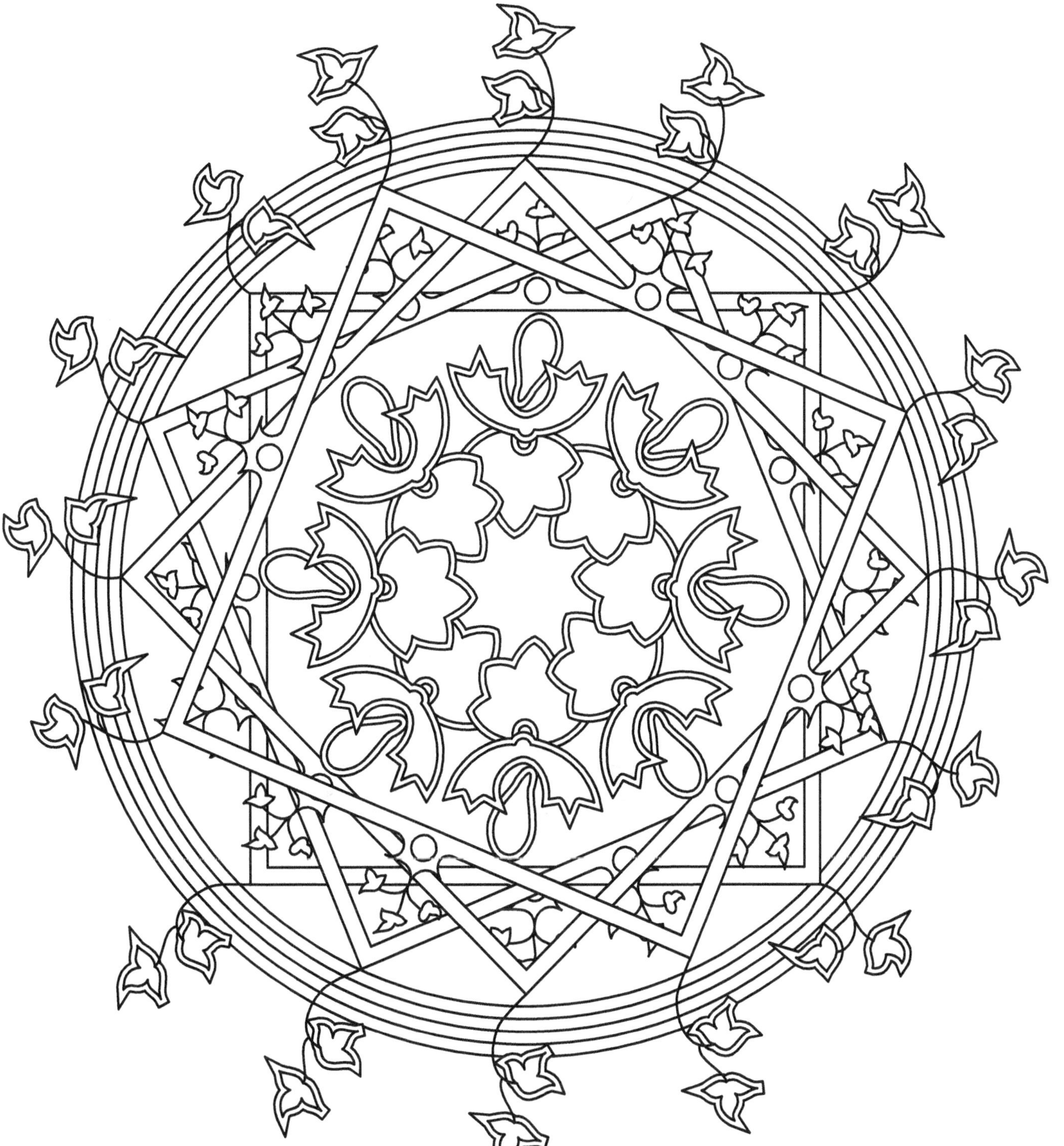

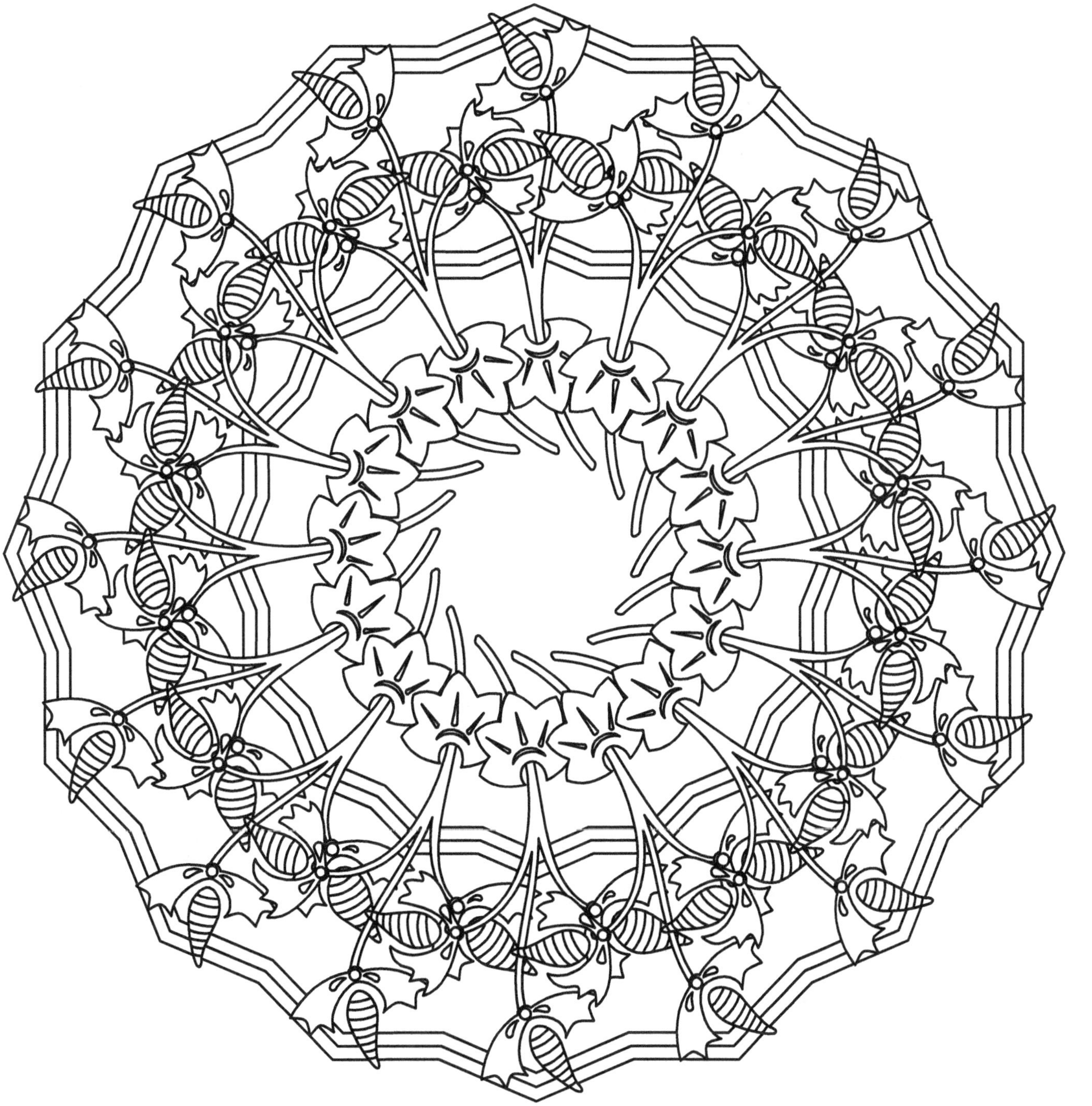

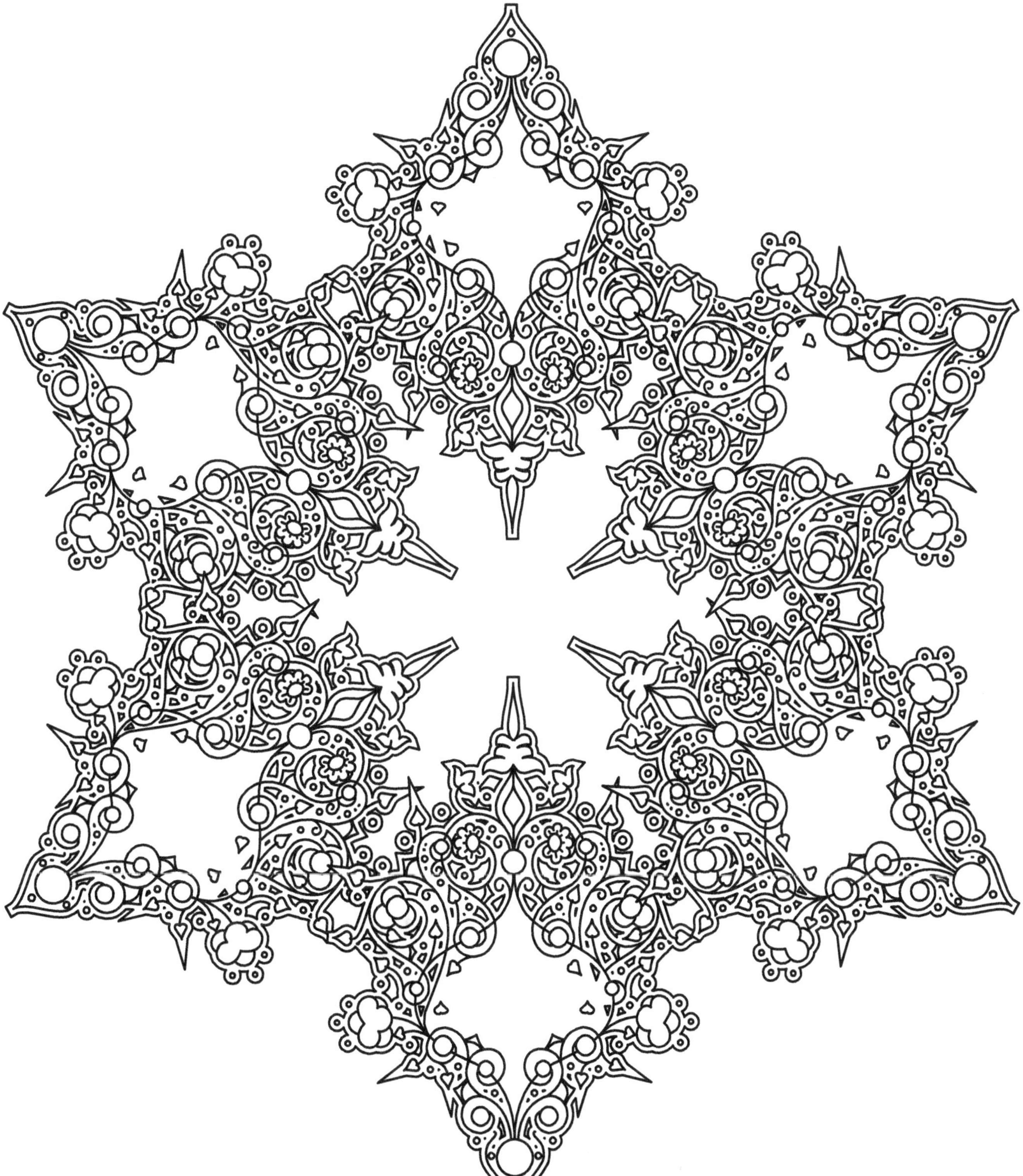

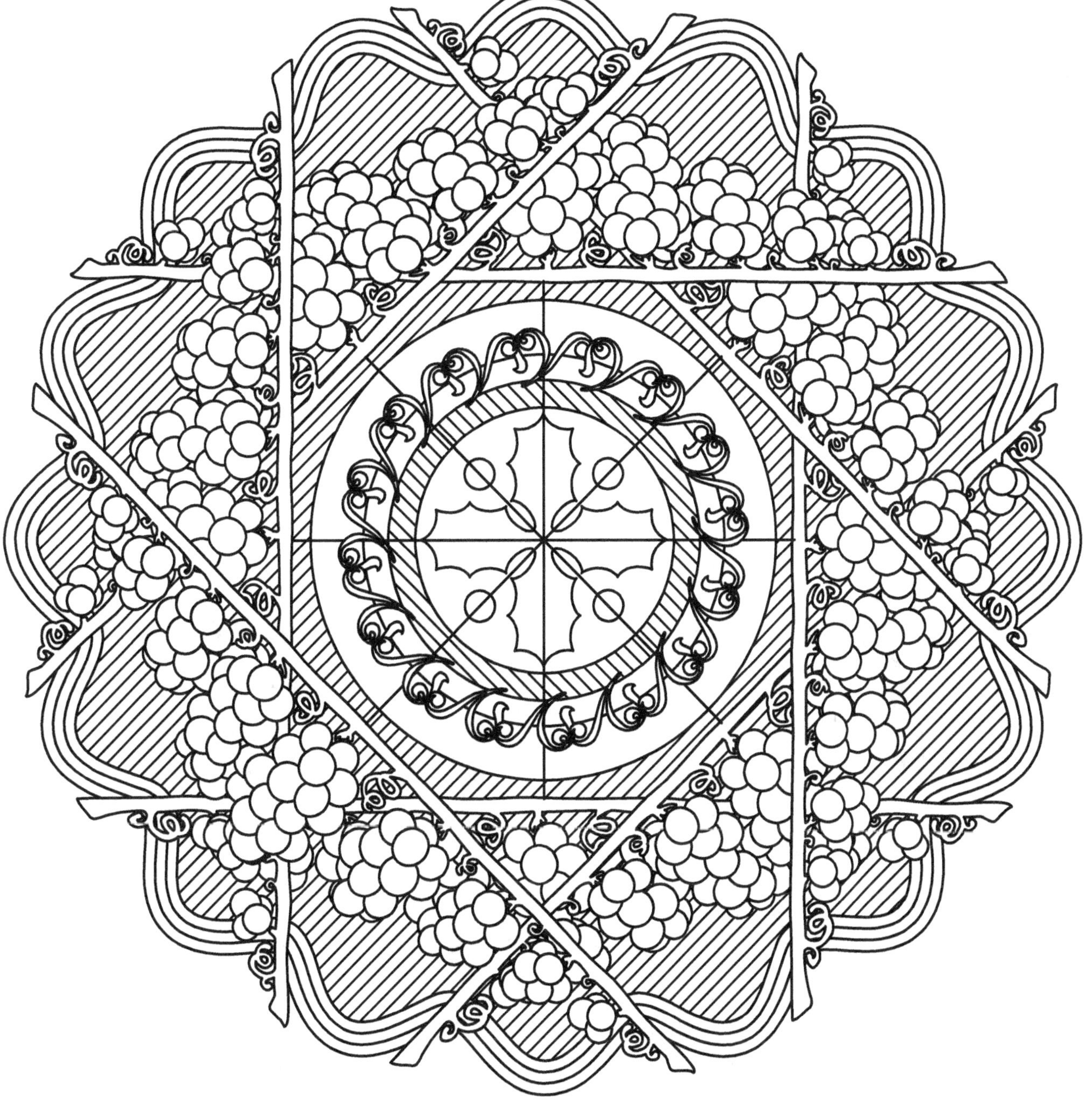

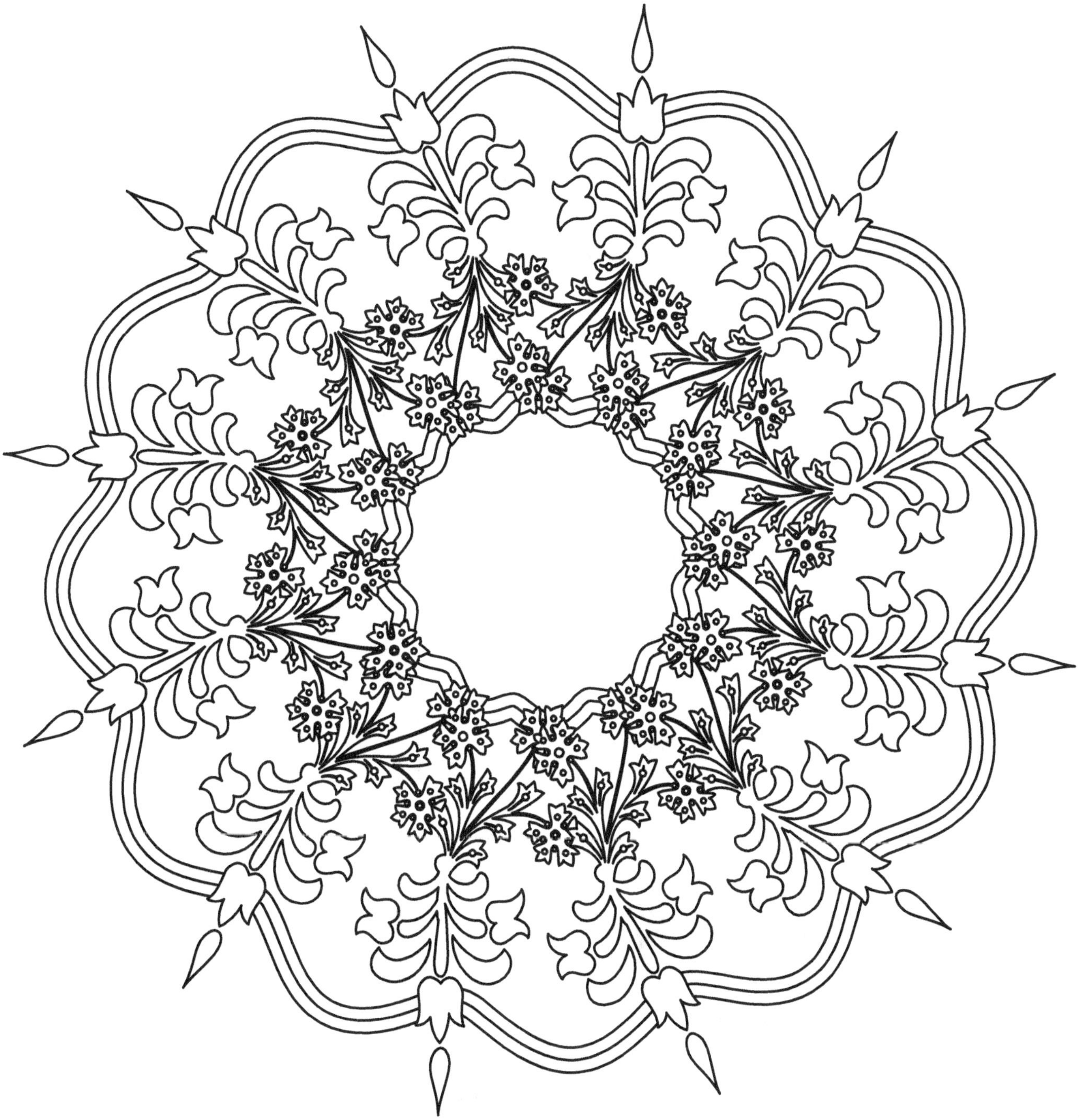

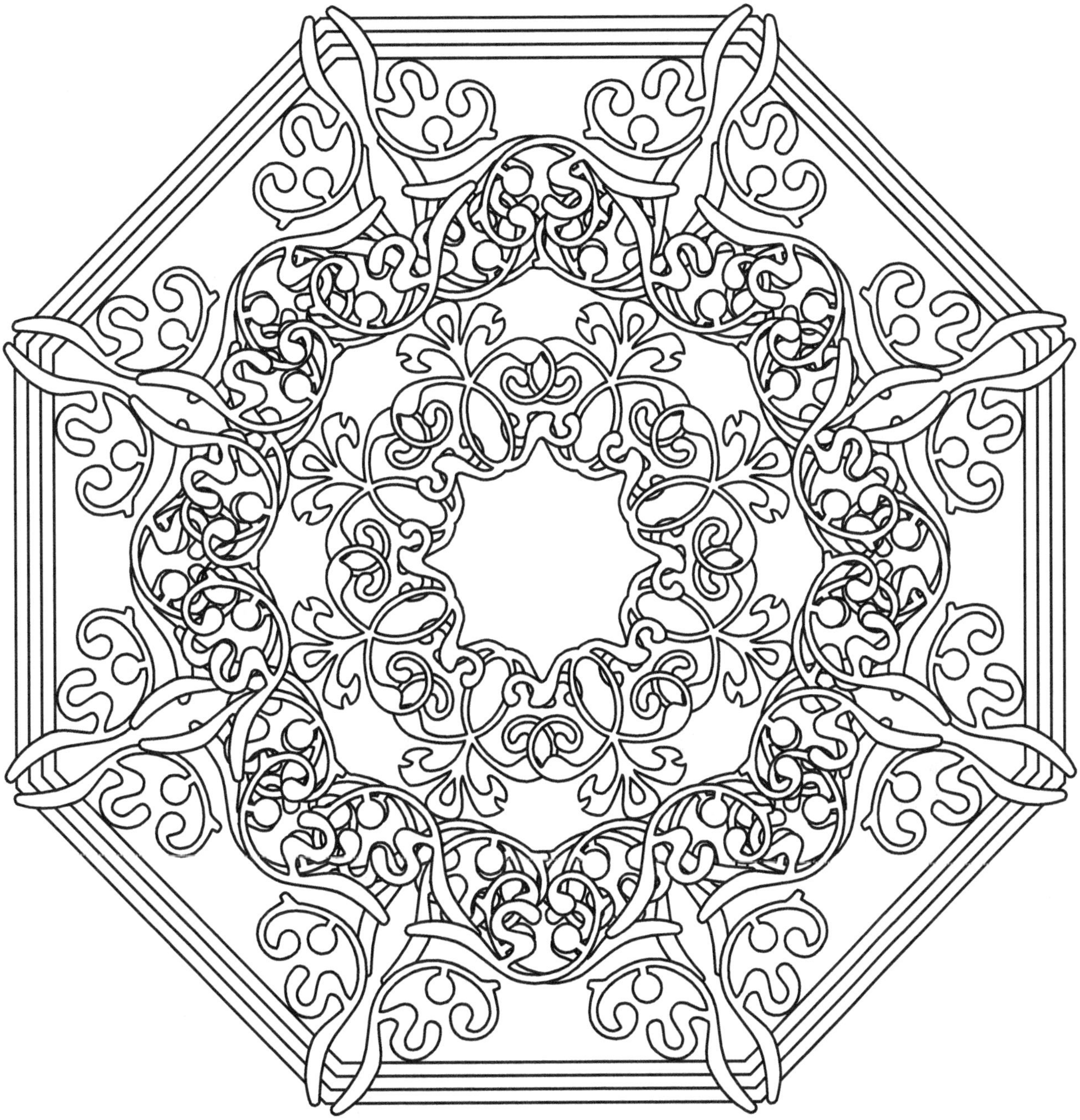

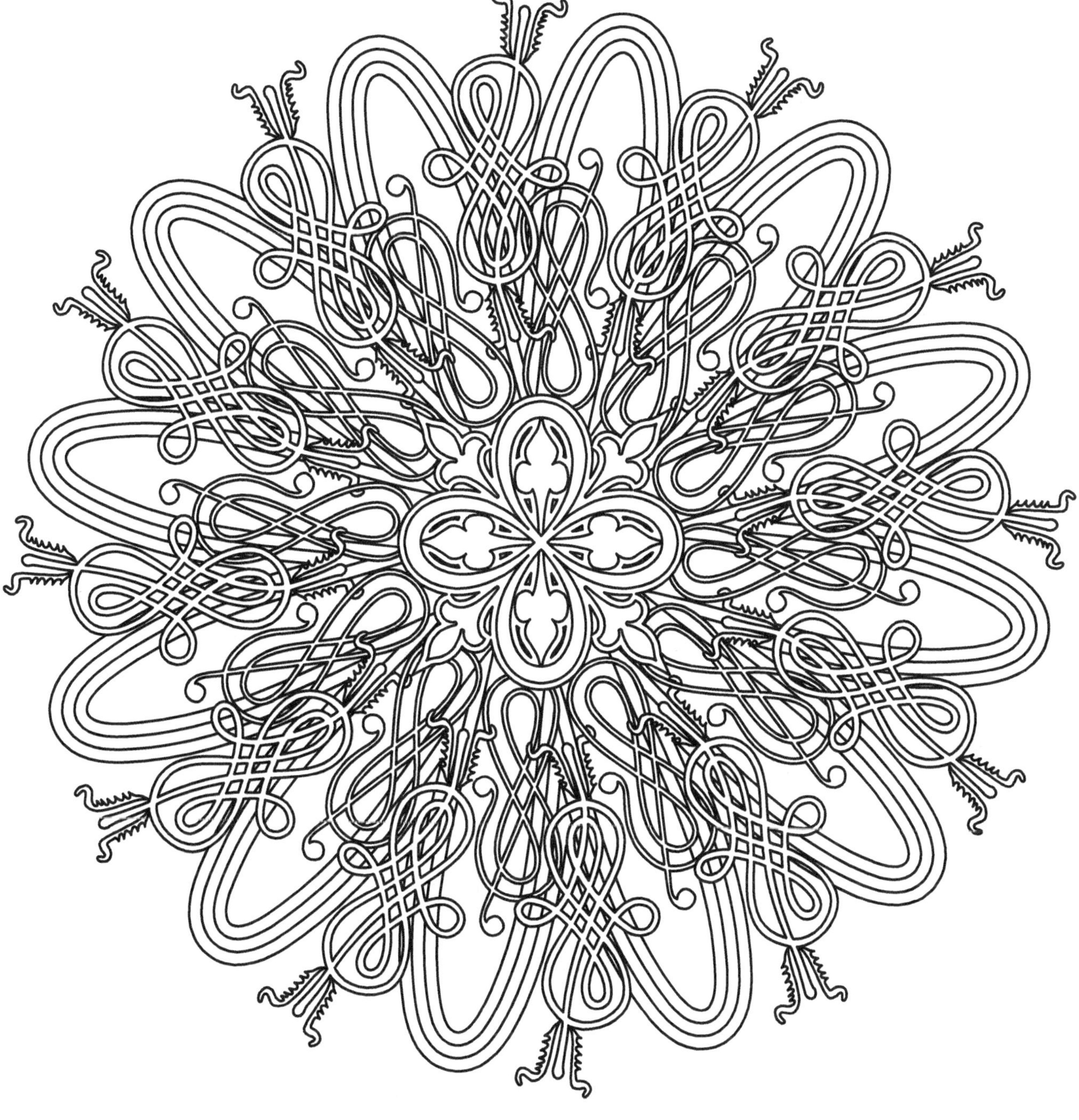

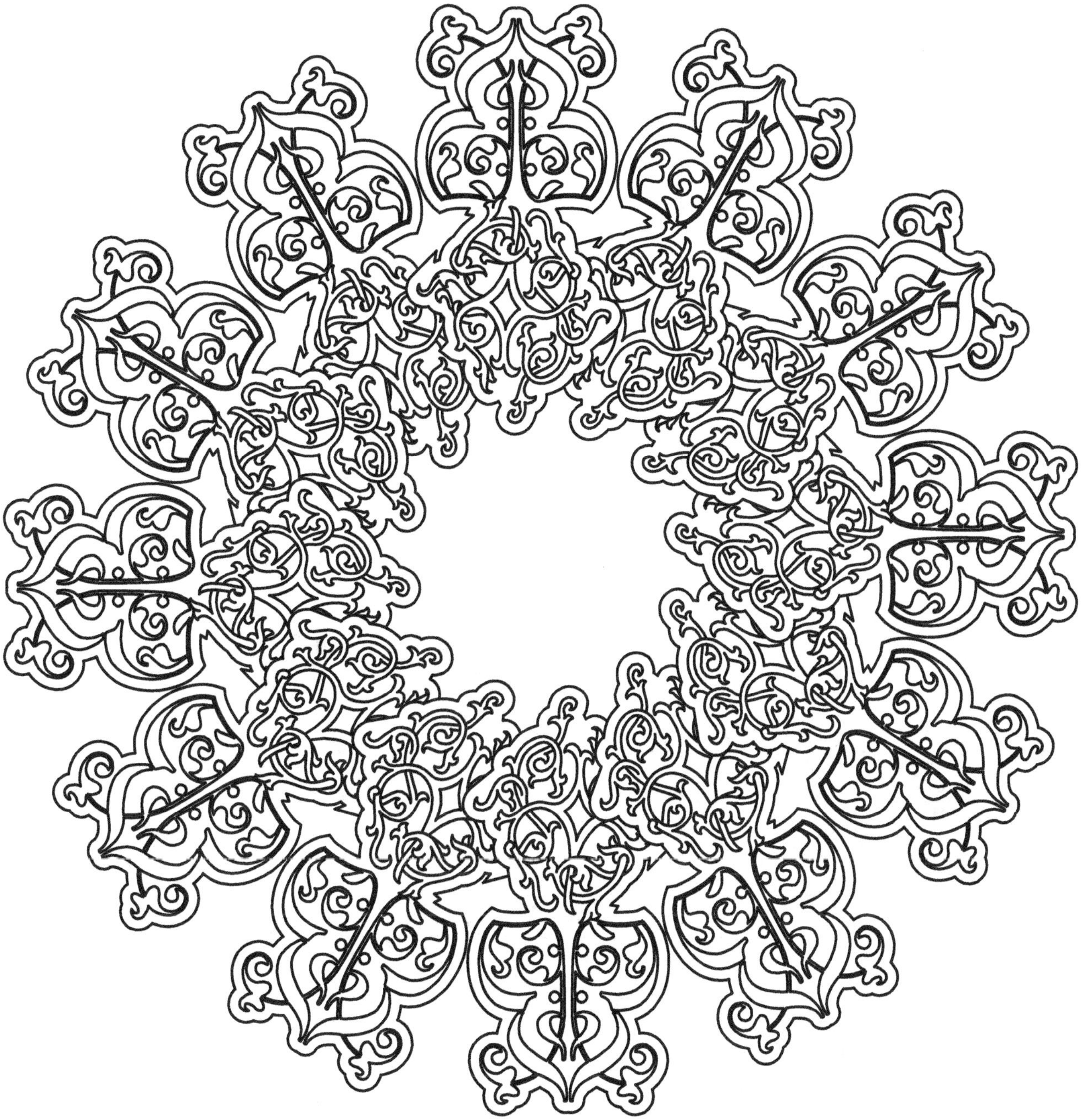

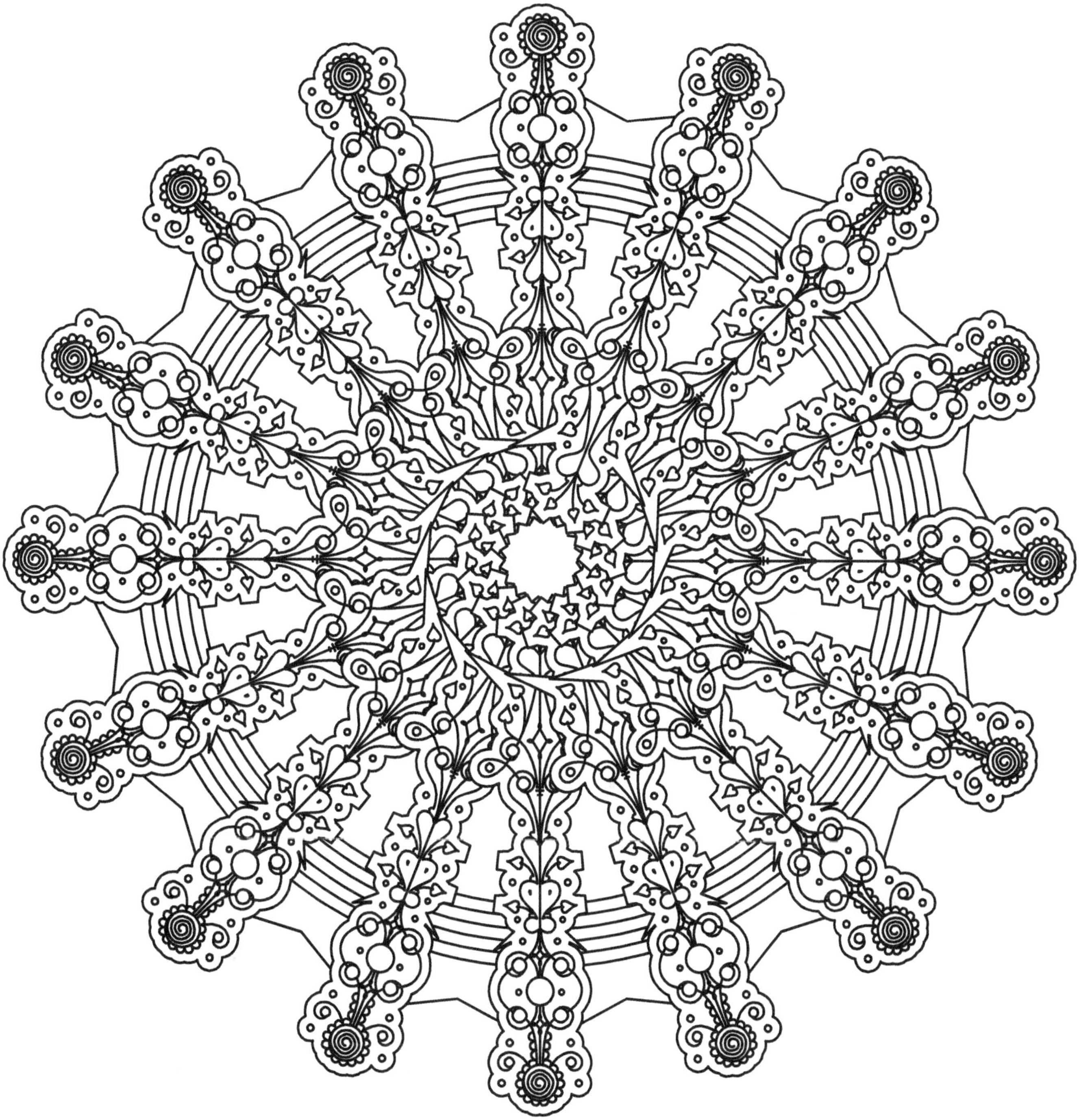

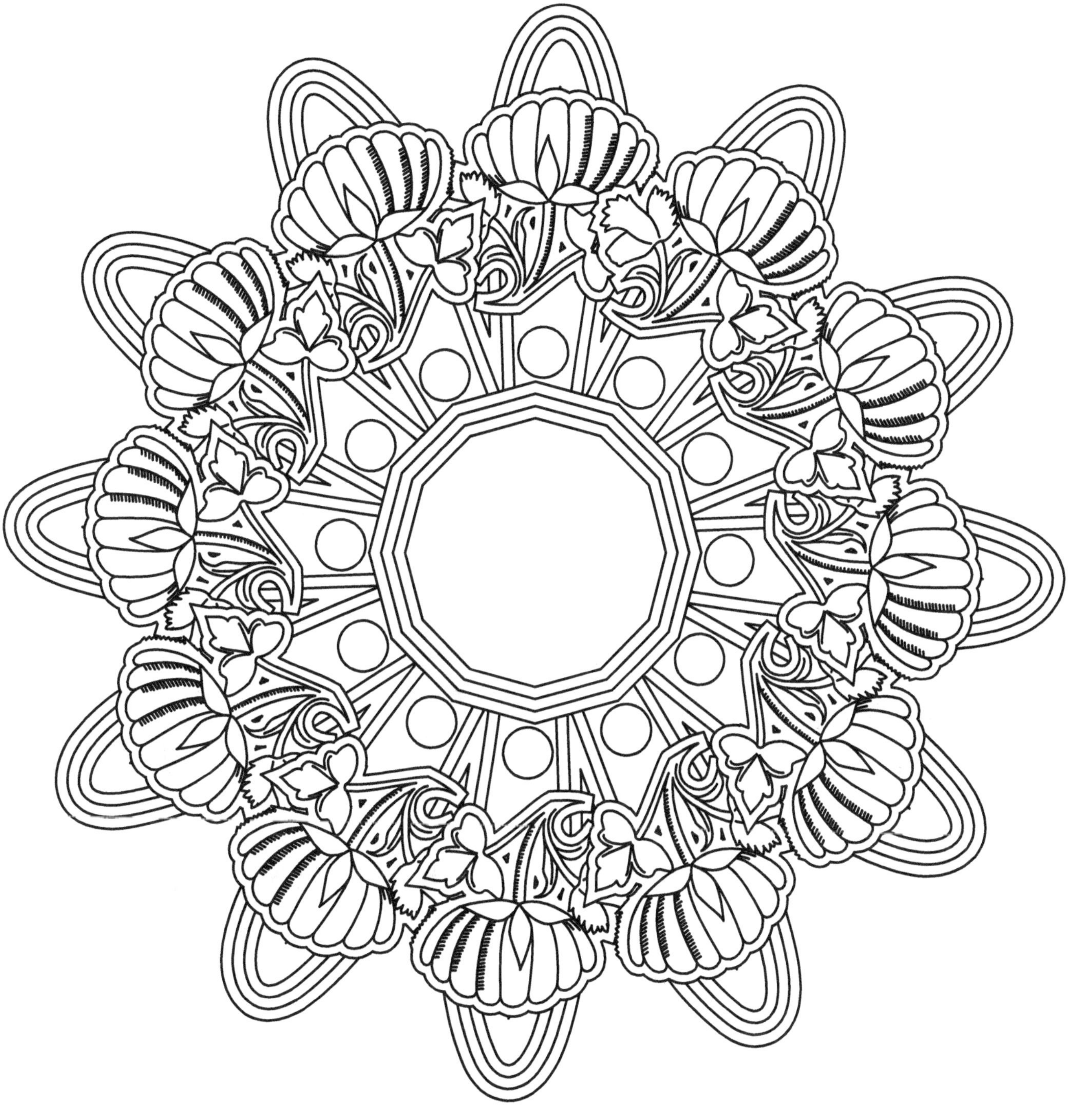

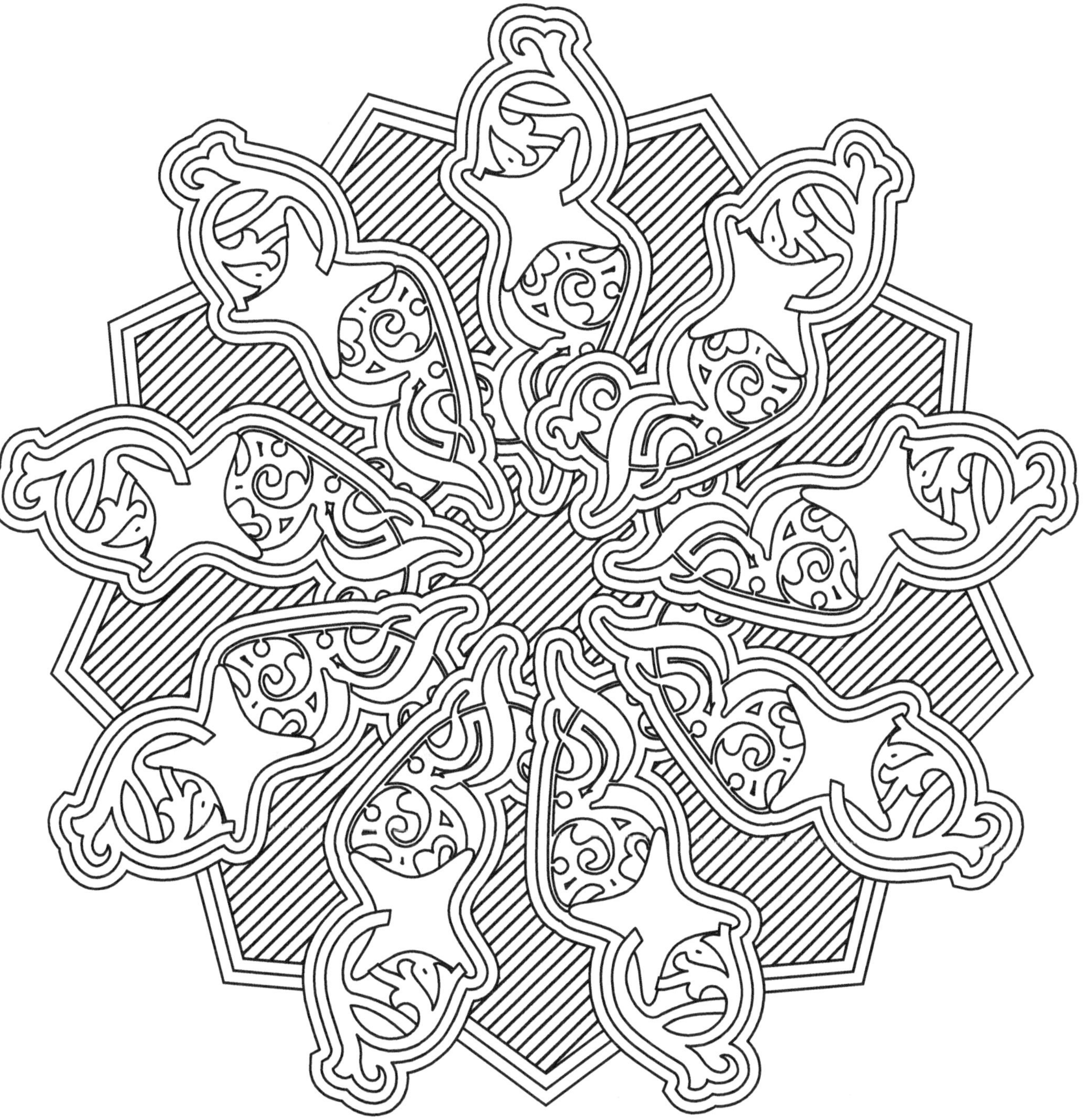

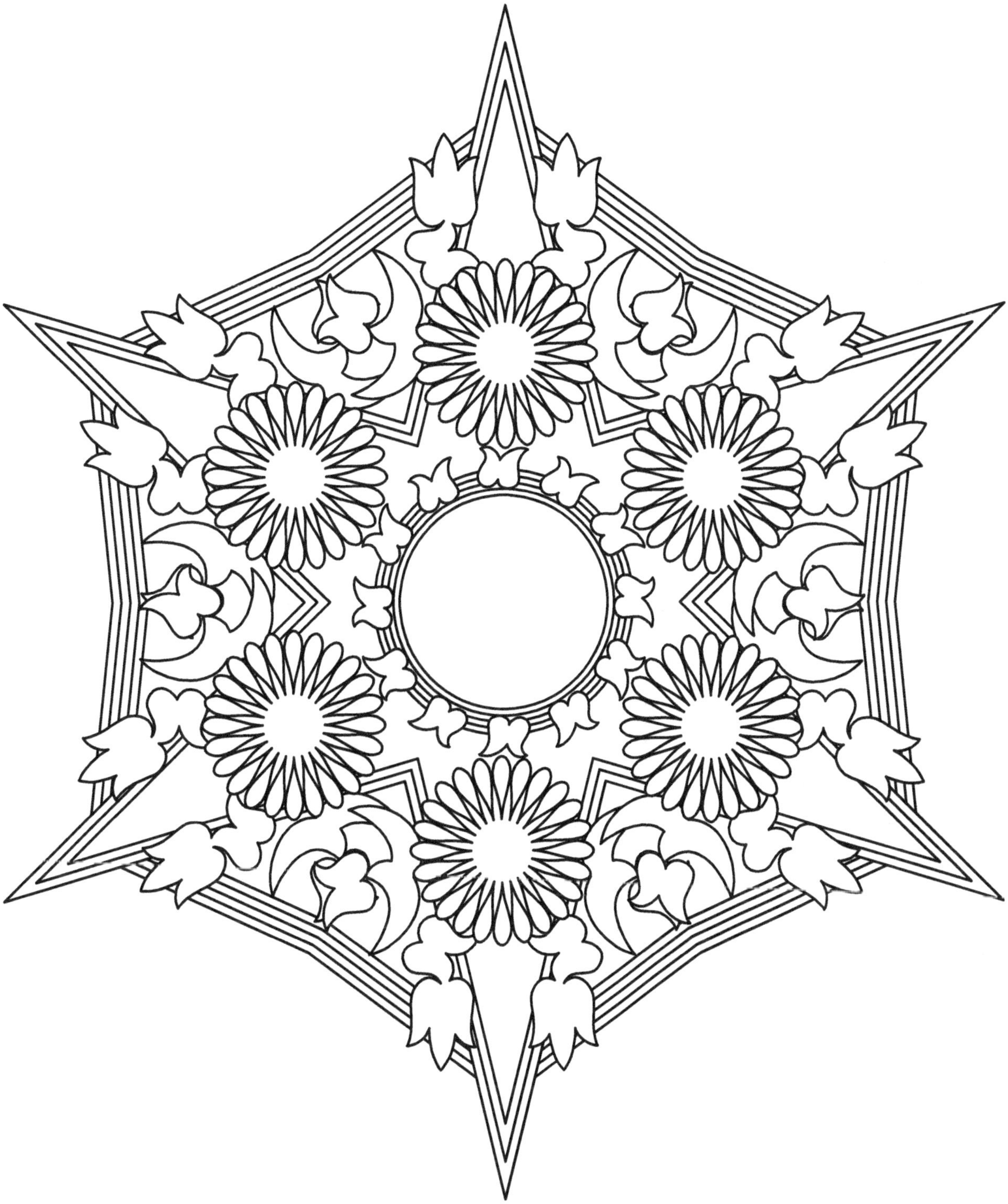

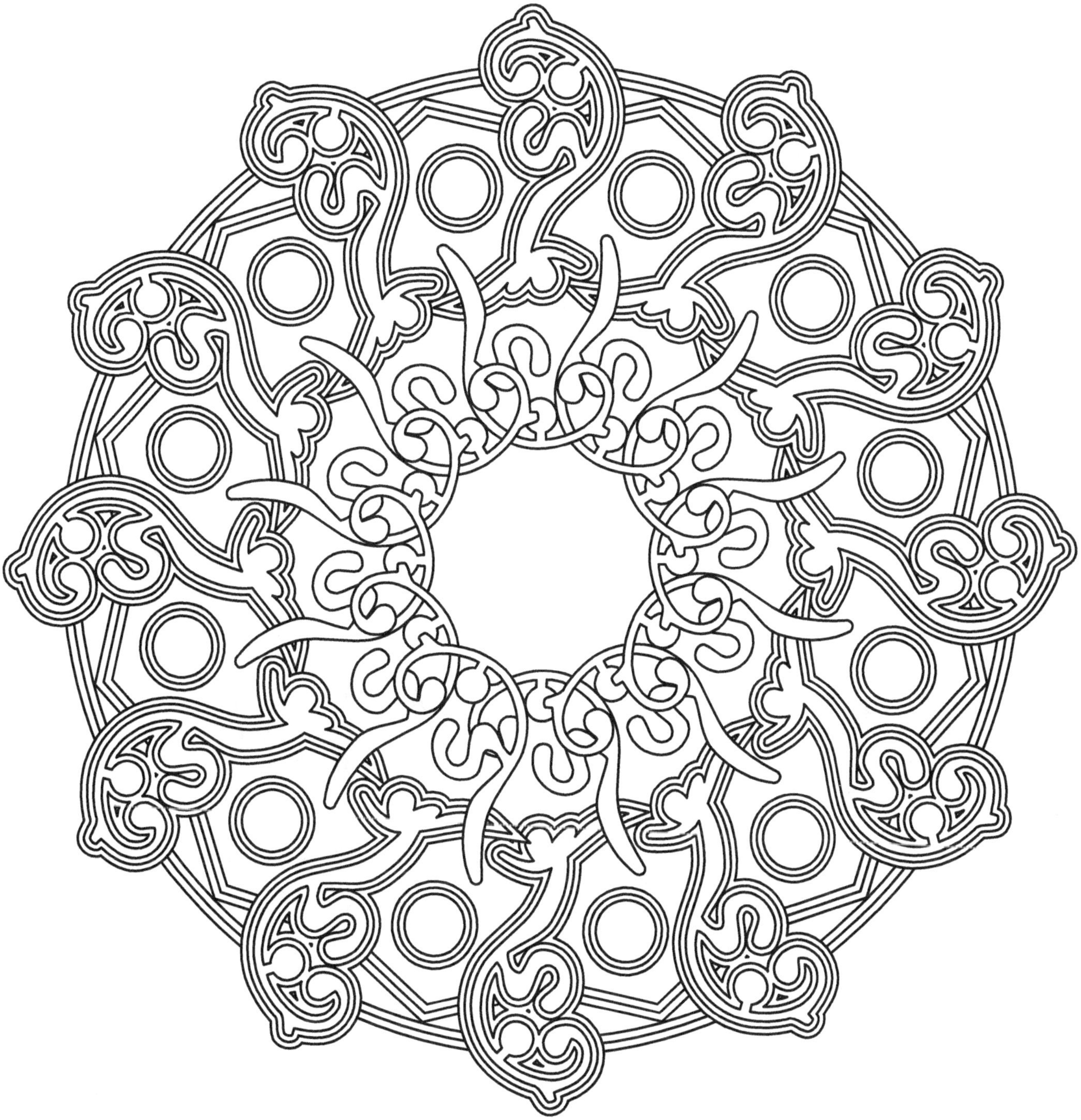

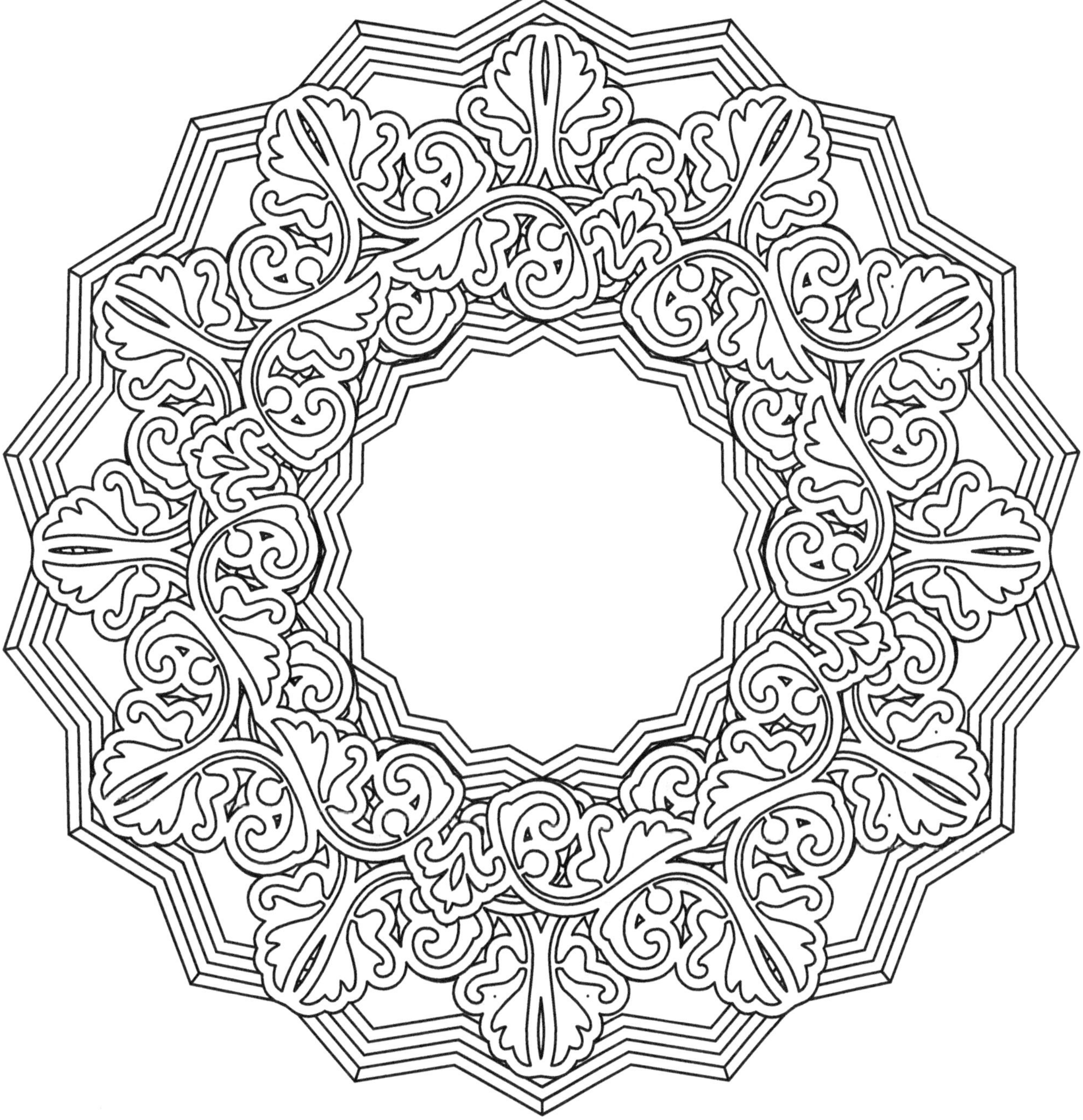

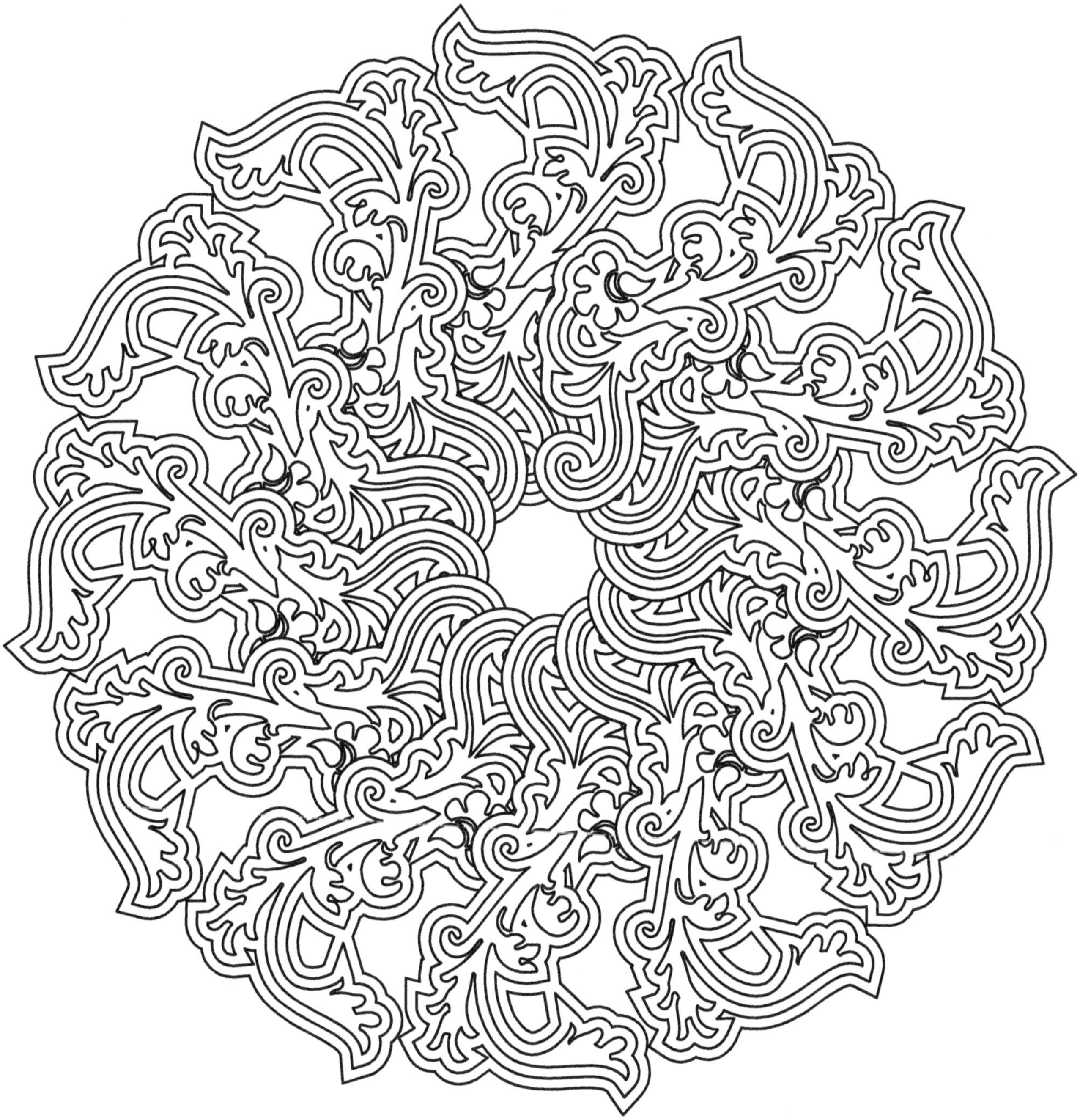

www.ingramcontent.com/pod-product-compliance
Lightning Source LLC
Chambersburg PA
CBHW060010210526
45170CB00017B/2145